INDIAN IDEALISM

Owing to the antiquity and rarity of this book, certain pages are regrettably absent, and readability is compromised due to the blurring of the original text. If you possess any insights regarding the availability of these missing sections, kindly inform us. Your assistance is crucial in ensuring the completion of this significant work for the benefit of future generations.

INDIAN IDEALISM

BY

SURENDRANATH DASGUPTA

M.A., Ph.D.

GYAN

Published by

Gyan Publishing House
5, Ansari Road
Daryaganj, New Delhi-110002
Phone: 011-47034999, 9811692060
E-mail: books@gyanbooks.com

Distribution Network
gyanbooks.com
India, USA, Canada, UK, Australia

ISBN: 978-93-6208-019-6 (HB)
First Published, 1933

2nd Impression 2024

Printed at: Gyan Press, Delhi.

INDIAN IDEALISM
Author: SURENDRANATH DAS GUPTA

INDIAN IDEALISM

INDIAN IDEALISM

BY

SURENDRANATH DASGUPTA
M.A., Ph.D.
PRINCIPAL, SANSKRIT COLLEGE, CALCUTTA
Author of *A History of Indian Philosophy*

CAMBRIDGE
AT THE UNIVERSITY PRESS
1933

DEDICATED

TO THE

REVERED MEMORY OF MY LOVING FATHER

KALIPRASANNA DASGUPTA

Contents

1. The emergence of philosophy from the ritualistic religion of the Vedas was a slow process, and even in its subsequent career philosophy in India has not become entirely free from the domination of religious tendencies.

2. Sacrifice became the most powerful instrument for securing one's desired ends and if duly performed it was bound to produce the desired results irrespective of the favour or disfavour of the gods, to whom it was ostensibly offered. The unalterable efficacy thus associated with the sacrificial acts came to be easily transferred to all acts and deeds in general, and so in this cult of sacrifice we find the germs of the law of Karma, which occupies such a central position of importance in the later ethico-philosophical speculations of India.

3. But bold philosophical speculations about the origin of the world from one God are not altogether wanting even in the Saṁhita period, and this is evidenced by some philosophical hymns of the Rigveda and the Atharvaveda, where for the first time the riddle of the universe is found to be attacked with wonderful philosophic insight and ability.

4. The magical value of the sacrificial deeds came to be transferred in course of time to meditation and to acts of self-mortification or *tapas* also, and the Purāṇas are full of stories of ascetics who achieve even impossible things by their tapas. But this is not a post-Vedic creation; it goes back even to Vedic times where we find it stated that the great Creator produced the world by an act of self-sacrifice or by performing tapas.

5. Two hymns from the Rigveda.

6. These hymns definitely prove that there were some minds at least among the Vedic seers who could rise, in spite of their predilections for sacrifice and tapas, to the conception of a Universal Creator, who held the destinies of the universe under His control. But this highest God is still an external God and has not yet come to be identified with our fundamental moral and spiritual existence. It is only in the Upanishads that the question of the Self and Brahman and their relation receives full consideration, and Brahman comes to be regarded not as an external deity but as the inmost reality of our being.

6. The question is raised whether the definition of idealism can be applied to the philosophical speculations of the Upanishads. The method of approach in the present work is entirely different from that of previous writers both in India and Europe and America.

7. The Kenopanishad describes Brahman as beyond the reach of words or thought, but at the same time it is the ultimate source from which all our powers and even the powers of gods are derived. Its nature is different from all that is known and all that is unknown, but one cannot find truth and become immortal unless one knows Brahman.

8. Though reminiscent of Brahman as the highest God, as in the Atharvaveda, the Brahman of the Kenopanishad is not an external deity, but is the inner controller of our thought and motor and sensory activities. It is the ultimate reality from which both the subject and the object derive their existence, and though beyond the reach of sensuous experience and logical thought, it can yet be somewhat realised. The philosophy of the Upanishad may therefore be regarded as a sort of mystical idealistic absolutism.

9. The Kaṭhopanishad describes the ultimate reality as invisible, all-pervading, yet hidden deep in the cave of the human heart. It is the inner essense of man, eternal and imperishable and unaffected by all bodily and mental changes. It can be realised through moral purity alone, and learning, scholarship or fine intellect are absolutely incompetent to reach it.

10. It is the great self of man and the ultimate essence of the world. One who fails to realise the essential unity of the world and thinks the manifold variety to be real is doomed. It is inconceivable and indescribable and can be realised as a mere be-ness, for all descriptions and predications fall outside.

11. A review of the philosophical ideas set forth in the Kaṭhopanishad. The ultimate reality is found to be spiritual, as the ground of all that is mental and all that is material. The Upanishad ends in mysticism when it refuses to define the ultimate reality, which in fact is unknowable and indescribable. The problem—how this reality can be the ground and source of our psychical life and of the multiform external world, and can yet remain unaffected by the modifications and changes going on therein—is left an unsolved mystery.

12. The Praśna Upanishad describes the individual as a bio-psychological entity composed of sixteen parts, which are all grounded in and derived from the inmost reality in us—the indestructible self.

13. The special point of interest of this Upanishad lies in its concentration on the nature of the bio-psychological individual, which is ultimately merged with all its individuality and specific characters in the highest self, like the waters of a river in the ocean. It is, however, unfortunately silent upon the nature of this highest reality as to whether

it is to be regarded as the inner essence of man or as a superior non-subjective spiritual entity.

14. The Muṇḍaka Upanishad starts with the enquiry into "what being known all else becomes known". It speaks of two sciences—the lower and the higher. The lower science consists of the study of the Vedas with their accessory literature, and the higher is that by which one realises the indestructible reality, the cause of all, from which all that exists comes out as a natural emanation. It further speaks of two selves, the higher and the lower, residing together on the tree of the human body, of which the former is free and pure and the lower is in bondage. When the lower self perceives the higher self as its lord it becomes free. It cannot be attained by those who are weak or inadvertent. The path of attainment is the path of knowledge and self-control.

15. The special feature of interest of the Muṇḍaka lies in its emphasis on the creation of the world as an emanation from Brahman, and here we notice its departure from the tradition of the Atharvaveda, where Brahman is looked upon as an external creator, the traces of which are still noticeable both in the Kena and the Kaṭha. The four similes used emphasise the fact that the world has sprung out of Brahman as a natural emanation. Brahman is described as omniscient, omnipotent and also as the self that resides in the heart of man. It does not, however, throw any light as to how the physical world can, with all its diverse forms and laws, be regarded as an emanation from the spiritual light which forms the inmost self in man. Apart from the classical interpretations, one way of reconciling the difficulty seems to regard Brahman as having two diverse manifestations, the one psychical and the other physical, which, however, do not represent its essential mystical nature, which is to be realised through the dawn of spiritual illumination. Viewed in this light thought and materiality would be like two attributes of Brahman—a philosophy closely akin to that of Spinoza.

16. The Māṇḍūkya speaks of the four stages of Brahman—the waking stage, the dream stage, the stage of dreamless sleep and the fourth stage, which is invisible, unthinkable and ungraspable. It is not described even as pure consciousness or bliss, but only in terms of pure negation. Here the philosophy of the Upanishads enters a new stage of development, and the negative description of the ultimate reality reminds one of Nāgārjuna's negativism, with this difference that here the stuff is described as ātman, whatever that may mean.

17. The chief importance of the Taittirīya Upanishad lies in its emphasis on the nature of Brahman as pure bliss, from which the whole world, conscious and unconscious, has come into existence. There are theistic passages which speak of Brahman as creating the world through tapas and as the sole controller of the forces of nature. The whole concept of creation through tapas seems to be pre-Upanishadic. Tapas is described as thought-activity in the Muṇḍaka, but this too does not make the

problem of creation easier of understanding. It remains a mystery how the world could come out of pure bliss or how Brahman, who is beyond thought, could take thought-activity as an instrument of creation.

18. The Chāndogya Upanishad speaks of Brahman as the ultimate reality from which everything is produced and to which everything returns. It is the subtle essence of all that exists, conscious and unconscious. Āruṇi says to his son Śvetaketu, "Thou art this subtle essence, which is identical with the universe". The Chāndogya emphasises the old truth that the ultimate reality is the subtle spiritual essence of man.

19. The most important contribution of the Chāndogya consists in its enunciation of the relation of cause and effect. It speaks of the cause as the essential reality and the effect as mere name and form. So, if the whole universe is to be viewed as being a transformation of Brahman, the ultimate reality can be affirmed of the causal stuff, Brahman alone. The view of the relation of the Universe with Brahman as formulated here seems to be entirely different from that of the Muṇḍaka, for in the latter the universe is looked upon as being a real transformation of Brahman as opposed to the *vivarta* view in the Chāndogya, where the material cause is the only reality and the transformations are mere illusory appearances.

20. The conception of Brahman as having two forms, visible and invisible, is not a new contribution of the Bṛhadāraṇyaka. Its notable contribution lies in the emphasis it lays upon the fact that the self is the dearest of all dear things—dearer than the son, riches and everything else—and that by discovery of this fact one attains the true bliss. This idea is brought into prominence in the dialogue between Maitreyī and Yājñavalkya where the latter explains that the self is the truest reality and everything else is true because of it. All differences are false and the ultimate reality is the undivided consciousness, which is the ground of all knowledge. It is beyond all predication and can be described only by negation of all that is knowable and predicable. It is the great self of man, the Brahman, the realisation of which gives immortality and ignorance of which means death.

21. Though the inner self is regarded as the ultimate reality and the multiplicity is denied, yet there is a passage which admits in a way the reality of the world by holding that the inner self of man is the inner controller of all the natural forces and phenomena. It is the eternal indwelling controller, the invisible seer, beyond which nothing exists.

22. The most important contribution of the Bṛhadāraṇyaka is the doctrine that the inmost self is of the nature of pure consciousness and pure bliss. All the knowledge and all the bliss of beings comes from this fountain head and are grounded in it as their ultimate cause of reality.

23. A résumé of the doctrines of the Upanishads and the fundamental features emphasised.

philosophy. It seems to be the best reconciliation of the apparently irreconcilable strands of thought found in the Upanishads. It gives a system of dynamic absolutism in which the Absolute, out of the necessity of its nature as thought, spontaneously moves itself through its will-power, called also time, and ultimately splits itself up into the subjective and the objective order.

8. The Upanishadic line of thought was followed by heretical schools of thought, who made bold adventures in independent thinking. The Ājīvakas are an instance in point. They denied the law of karma and set up a sort of ethical nihilism. The next phase of development was marked by the rise of Buddhism and Jainism, who entered an emphatic protest against the fatalism of the Ājīvakas.

9. The life and career of Gautama Buddha.

10. Buddha preached the doctrine of the twelvefold chain of causation. The doctrines of a permanent self and permanent substance were denied.

11. The true self of the Upanishads was a matter of transcendental experiences, but this was denied by the Buddha, who regarded the idea of a permanent self in any form as a delusion.

12. The early phase of Buddhism was a system of pluralistic phenomenalism with neither matter nor mind as abiding entities.

13. It is a matter of much speculative interest as to how this doctrine could give rise to systems of monism, idealism or absolutism in later periods in the hands of Brahmin converts who had probably a grounding in the Upanishads.

1. The doctrine of the unsubstantiality and the impermanence of all elements of existence was pushed to its logical consequence of nihilism by Nāgārjuna, who applied the Law of Contradiction to all phenomena and concepts and showed that they could be explained neither by themselves nor by others and hence were essenceless appearances.

2. Nāgārjuna's definition of reality as that which does not depend on anything else for its existence was applied to all phenomena, and as they were found to have no self-existence they were declared to be illusory appearances. *Nirvāṇa* is said to bring about the cessation of phenomena, but in reality they never existed. Even the Buddha and his teaching are in reality mere appearances, like a mirage or a dream or the illusory snake in the rope.

3. The division of things into phenomenal and metaphysical order. In the phenomenal plane it is content to follow the commonsense logic of the Naiyāyikas and looks upon the logical and epistemological improvements of Diṅnāga's school as futile and wrong. In the metaphysical order, it has no thesis, as it does not tolerate any kind of essence or reality

behind the phenomenal order. Its philosophy is therefore neither idealism nor realism nor even absolutism but pure phenomenalism.

4. The philosophy of *bhūtatathatā* of Aśvaghosha, together with the Laṅkāvatāra, marks the foundation of Buddhist idealism. The *tathatā* means the oneness of all things whose essential nature is uncreative and eternal. It appears as subject and object owing to the working of incipient, unconscious memory (*vāsanā*) of our past experiences.

5. The *tathatā* can be realised by pure wisdom, when the integrated constitution of the mind through associations and relations is broken down and the modes of evolving consciousness will be annulled. This is possible because it is pure, eternal, calm and immutable in its true nature.

6. Enlightenment and non-enlightenment. The three ways of the manifestation of non-enlightenment and the consequent rising of the phenomenal world and the reaction of the subjective consciousness.

7. The relation between truth and *avidyā*.

8. The working of *avidyā* on the all-pervading consciousness and the evolution of the ego with its various faculties and functions and the ego-creation of the external world.

9. Non-enlightenment is the *raison d'être* of birth and rebirth. *Nirvāṇa* is the annihilation of the modes of the mind and not of the mind itself. The theory of inter-perfuming as an explanation of the interaction and inter-relation of *tathatā*, *avidyā* and *vishaya* (the external world).

10. *Nirvāṇa* is not nothingness but *tathatā* in its purity with the veil of ignorance removed.

11. Aśvaghosha's philosophy compared and contrasted with the philosophy of the Upanishads and of early Buddhism. *Avidyā* is given a new orientation. The comprehensive character of Aśvaghosha's philosophy, which may be characterised as Subjective idealism, Pure absolutism and also as Absolute idealism when viewed from different angles of vision.

12. The idealism of the Laṅkāvatāra. The external world is a creation of consciousness with its two functions induced by the beginningless *avidyā*.

13. The ultimate reality is described as "thatness" in one place and as "voidness" in another place, which is one and has no origin or essence. It cannot be characterised as a positive entity, which would be equated with Vedāntic Brahman. It is a stage in which the positive and the negative coincide.

14. *Pratītyasamutpāda*, both external and internal, and the world of matter are false appearances, created by the twofold faculty of our understanding.

existence of the external objective world and ends in affirmation of oneness of all things.

3. The difference of perception and memory explained, and the difficulty of intercommunication and uniformity of experiences solved by the theory of direct action of one subjectivity upon another subjectivity. The evolution of the subjective and objective categories, the individual perceivers and the objects perceived, are held to be the self-creation of one thought-principle. The transformation of the self-evolving thought is regarded as real by Vasubandhu as opposed to Aśvaghosha, who believes such transformations to be illusory appearances.

4. The mode of causation allowed by Vasubandhu is that of *pratītyasamutpāda*, which holds that the effect is a novel phenomenon distinct from the cause, which comes into being independently of an external excitant cause. It is entirely different from the *pariṇāma* (transformation) of the Sāṃkhya school, which means that the effects produced are but transformations which were already existent in a latent form in the causal substance, but this presupposition is denied by Vasubandhu.

5. The first two forms of transformation of the *ālayavijñāna*, of which the initial change is called *vipāka* (the accumulation of the results of past root-instincts), and the second again is of two kinds, *manana* (psychosis) and *vishayavijñapti* (perceptive character). The ālayavijñāna is called such because it is the home of the seeds or root-instincts that lead to world-experiences. It manifests itself as the internal psychosis or microcosm and as the external world of Space. The ālayavijñāna contains within itself the elements of subjectivity and externality in an undifferentiated form and is a dynamic principle, splitting itself up into different subjective centres, which acquire fresh experiences and produce fresh instincts and are again reacted upon by these tendencies. With regard to the enlightened subject, the ālayavijñāna ceases to work and is lost in the ground consciousness.

6. The third transformation is in the form of perception of six classes of objects, colour, sounds, etc., which are determined by the antecedent moments as their causes. The different cognitions are but impositions upon the nature of consciousness and have no existence outside it. The ālayavijñāna as conceived by Vasubandhu is different from that of Aśvaghosha, the latter being a differenceless entity, whereas the former is a dynamic concrete universal thought-principle which by an act of self-alienation externalises itself as the world of objects. The three kinds of essencelessness of these appearances described.

7. The *ālayavijñāna* is the ground of all individual centres of experience analogous to the *buddhitattva* of the Sāṃkhya, containing the resultant tendencies of the whole past. It is one unitary principle from which the individual subjects spring out and in which the past and future

experiences are gathered up as root-tendencies, making the further future career of individuals possible.

8. The *ālayavijñāna* so conceived is but a hypothetical state and is grounded upon the foundation of pure consciousness, which is also of the nature of pure bliss, eternal, transcendent, unchangeable and unthinkable in character like the Brahman of the Vedānta. The close similarity of Vasubandhu's philosophy to the Vedānta of Śaṅkara's school discussed and fully brought out.

9. Maitreya and Asaṅga gave an idealistic philosophy closely akin to the philosophy of Vasubandhu in their work called Madhyantavibhaṅga, which was commented upon by Vasubandhu and Sthiramati. So Vasubandhu was not the originator of this type of philosophy. It however appears to have been influenced by the logic of the Laṅkāvatāra. The subjective thought and the objective reality are held to be false alike together with their relations. But it does not end in pure negation as the ultimate truth, as that would preclude the possibility of illusion.

10. The three forms of appearances. It admits the existence of one pure consciousness absolute and eternal, entrance into which brings salvation.

11. The doctrine of causation in the Theravāda school. Two causal categories, *paccaya* and *paṭṭhāna*. The former stands for those causal conditions which can transmit their energy to the effects. Twenty-four kinds of paṭṭhāna. The two kinds of *pratyaya-samutpāda*—one due to *hetu* and another due to *pratyayas* as propounded in the Śālistambhasūtra. This view of causation denies the necessity of any kind of relation between cause and effect and reduces it to mere succession.

12. Candrakīrti's interpretation of causal relation in the commentary on Nāgārjuna's Mādhyamika Kārikā. The relation of cause and effect is logically indeterminable appearance.

13. Relations are proved to be imaginary constructions by Śāntarakshita and Kamalaśīla. Difference of qualities and substances is a false creation of the understanding. So also are the universals.

14. The datum of perception is a unique and indescribable fact, which is made determinate by the application of categories of quality, quantity, relation, etc., which by themselves have no reality and are external to the unique real. The association of categories is a post-perceptual act of imaginative tendencies.

15. In the Buddhist idealism as interpreted by Śāntarakshita, the objects have no independent existence from their awareness. The objective reference is a false projection. The question of validity or invalidity of our experiences in this view reduces itself to a question of self-consistency or inconsistency.

16. Śāntarakshita refutes the existence of external objects by attacking the atomic theory after the fashion of Vasubandhu, but his difference

from Vasubandhu's idealism is also fundamental in that he denies the existence of one eternal conscious principle such as *vijñaptimātratā*, which is the ultimate category with the former. Śāntarakshita's idealism is pluralistic and not monistic like that of Vasubandhu.

17. The doctrine of *pudgala* as the principle of individuality both different from and identical with the combining elements, which is postulated by the Vātsīputrīyas and the Sammitīyas, is scouted as unphilosophical and self-contradictory.

18. The heretical doctrines of permanent selves and the existence of the external world as a conglomeration of atoms are refuted by the exposure of self-contradiction inherent in such conceptions. The ultimate conclusion is the existence of diverse centres of consciousness, each constituting a series by itself, in which there is a perpetual succession of one moment of consciousness by another, each distinct from the other and self-revelatory in character.

19. The identity of knowledge and its object is proved by the law of simultaneous manifestation of the object and its awareness. This simultaneity is impossible of explanation except on the supposition of their identity. But this identity does not imply that consciousness is changed into the forms of objects or that objects are petrified consciousness. The objects as forms of consciousness are purely illusory manifestations.

20. Śāntarakshita does not believe in one eternal ground-consciousness and also denies the *ālayavijñāna* as a concrete universal in which the different centres of consciousness are synthesised and integrated. This distinguishes his philosophy from the idealism of Vasubandhu.

21. Śāntarakshita repudiates the Nyāya theory of a permanent self as the unifying principle of our psychological experience, on the ground of self-contradiction and infinite regression inevitable in such conception. The idea of a unitary self is an illusion.

22. The Sāṃkhya view of the self as pure consciousness and its theory of vicarious enjoyment, though the functions of the *buddhi* are equally untenable owing to the difficulty of relations between them.

23. The Upanishadic conception of one eternal consciousness cannot be maintained on account of its failure to explain the diversity of experiences. It also fails to explain the distinction of true knowledge from false knowledge and makes bondage and emancipation impossible.

24. Buddhist denial of a permanent self on the ground of consciousness being a product of psychological elements. It is criticised by Śaṅkara.

25. Śāntarakshita's definition of reality as its capacity for serving a purpose leads to the doctrine of momentariness of things.

26. The objections based on recognition of identity and sameness of nomenclature are proved to be invalid.

9. The appearance of successive categories does not imply any change in the being of pure consciousness, and the act of self-alienation is an illusory appearance. The experience of the world-order is as fictitious as dream constructions.

10. The difference between our wakeful experience and dream experience is one of degree and not of kind. The former has more consistency, apparent persistence and continuity, whereas the latter is of short duration. They are at bottom equally false creations of the imaginative activity of *manas*.

11. The striking similarity of the Philosophy of the Yogavāsishṭha with the idealistic systems of Vasubandhu and others. If *manas* be equated with the *ālayavijñāna* of Vasubandhu, it would be difficult to distinguish the two systems.

12. Bādarāyaṇa seems to advocate the doctrine of Bhedābhedavāda, in which the immanence and transcendence of Brahman are equally emphasised. This philosophy is earlier than the absolute monism of Śaṅkara, as is evident from Śaṅkara's references to the views of Bhartṛprapañca and the Vṛttikāra which advocated some form of *bhedābhedavāda*.

13. Though it is difficult to define the exact character of the *bhedābhedavāda* entertained by Bādarāyaṇa, it is almost certain that he regards the causal transformations of Brahman as real. Even Śaṅkara could not point out a sūtra which supported the vivarta view. This and the diversity of views among post-Śaṅkara writers about the specific causality of Brahman show that Śaṅkara's interpretation was not above question.

14. Śaṅkara starts with his theory of illusion by reason of which the self as pure consciousness is identified with body and mind and behaves as an individual. His theory of illusion follows as a corollary from the Upanishadic monism, which he accepts without proof and without question. The world of experience, with all its diversity and plurality, which is in antagonism with the conception of Pure consciousness, the only reality, is simply thrown overboard as the creation of *māyā*.

15. Brahman is the ultimate cause of the world, and as the ultimate cause it must be intelligent, otherwise the law and order of the world could not be explained. It is also the inmost essence of us all—the immediate consciousness that shines as the self and expresses the objects of cognition.

16. Brahman, according to Śaṅkara, is the identity of pure being, intelligence and pure bliss and is the true self of us all. Its nature is partially realised in dreamless sleep. Creation of a diverse world is the work of *māyā*, which is equally illusory with its products. Brahman in association with māyā seems to be the creator, as both the material and the efficient causes of the world, and as effects are but illusory super-impositions upon the causer, the world is also a super-imposition upon Brahman and has no existence by itself.

17. The twofold view of things in Vedānta—one referring to the ultimate reality and the other to appearance. The ultimate reality is pure intelligence, which is changeless and devoid of subject distinctions. In all the varied experiences the self as pure consciousness remains unchanged and the change and diversity belong to the contents. This is proved by an analysis of the epistemological situation involved in all experiences.

18. Consciousness is the fact of revelation—which is one in all experiences. The distinctions of time and space, quality and quantity and the like are out of the question with regard to consciousness.

19. Consciousness as revelation cannot be characterised either as a fact or as an act. It is one unchangeable entity which reveals all finite things, but there is no finitude in it. The "I" is as much a content as any other object. Revelation cannot be individuated and all distinctions of "I" or "thou" or "mine", etc. fall outside of it. All existence can be divided under two heads—the principle of revelation and all that is revealed. The former is eternal, unchangeable, absolute and all-pervading consciousness, and the latter is constituted of an unsubstantial, indefinable stuff called *māyā*.

20. In the Dṛṣṭi-sṛṣṭi school of Śaṅkara Vedānta, it is held that all is pure and simple illusion, and that things exist only when they are perceived; and dissolve into nothingness as soon as we cease to perceive them. Prakāśānanda, following Maṇḍana, the original expounder of this school, argues in trenchant dialectic that there is no proof that cognition and cognised objects are different.

21. Prakāśānanda, however, does not attempt to give any positive proof in support of his thesis that the world-appearance and all objects contained in it have no existence while they are not perceived, or that the being of all objects cognised is their *percipi*. He only tried to show that it could not be logically established that the cognised objects were different from their cognition.

22. The idealism of Śaṅkara and that of Vasubandhu compared. In the former the basic principle of pure intelligence explains the growth of experience in each individual; while in Vasubandhu's system the ultimate consciousness, necessary as an unchangeable background of all the changes of ordinary experience, remains in its undisturbed quiescence.

23. Padmapāda points out that the main point with the Buddhist is his doctrine of causal efficiency; and he refutes this by arguing that if causal efficiency means the production of another moment, then the last moment, having no other moment to produce, would itself be non-existent, with the consequence that all other moments would be non-existent.

24. Pure consciousness, associated with the mind and memory-impressions, gives rise to the category of ego-consciousness, which by itself is a fiction.

37. The concrete idealism of the Śaiva schools is a later development from Śaṅkara Vedānta. The main point of departure lies in the unification of consciousness and *māyā*, which together constitute one concrete reality. Māyā is the real energy of the Absolute and not an unreal adjunct as in Vedānta.

38. The Kāshmira school of idealism, as developed by Abhinavagupta and others, though closely analogous to Śaṅkara Vedānta, differs from the latter in its conception of the ultimate reality. The ultimate principle is pure consciousness endowed with self-spontaneity, and it is this self-spontaneous consciousness which manifests itself as psychological categories and as objective data side by side, and this makes the whole world of mind and matter with all their developments essentially spiritual in nature.

39. Śaṅkara's obligation to previous philosophers, notably to the Buddhists. The *vivartavāda* (the theory of illusory causation) and the consequent denial of pluralism, which may be regarded as original contributions, were also anticipated by Bhartrihari.

40. The theistic systems of thought, which may be regarded as idealistic from one point of view or another, have however been left out of account in the present work, for their pronounced realistic sympathies. The dominant position of idealism in all branches of Indian thought and its influence on Indian ideology and life cannot be overestimated.

Preface

Years ago these Lectures were delivered as the Readership Lectures of the Patna University. Their publication has been delayed for various circumstances over which I had no control. This is probably the first attempt to put together some of the most important strands of Indian idealistic thought within a small compass. I fear however that my success has been but a doubtful one. The field of Indian Idealism is very vast and defies any attempt at compression. The table of contents will, I hope, be found helpful in following the general argument of the different chapters. These Lectures are printed here more or less in the same form in which they were delivered. Conscious as I am of my shortcomings and defects, I feel that they would have been far greater had it not been for the help that was rendered me in reading the proofs of these Lectures by my esteemed friend Mr Haridas Bhattacharyya, M.A., P.R.S., of the University of Dacca. I am also grateful to my esteemed pupils, Dr Satkari Mukherjee, M.A., Ph.D., of the Calcutta University for the preparation of their contents, and to Mr Satindra Kumar Mukherjee, M.A., and Miss Surama Mitra, M.A., for the assistance I received from them, without which, in my present state of health, it would have been wellnigh impossible for me to see the book through the press.

S. N. DASGUPTA.

SANSKRIT COLLEGE
CALCUTTA
5th April 1933

Chapter I

BEGINNINGS OF INDIAN PHILOSOPHY

1. Indian philosophy has slowly emerged from the briny waters of the ritualistic religion of the Vedas, and though in later times it could very largely concentrate on problems which may be deemed purely philosophical, yet it could not at any time completely dissociate itself from religious tendencies. The Rigveda consists mainly of hymns dedicated to Nature-Gods, such as the fire, the sun, the dawn, Indra, the God of rains, etc., and there is sometimes much poetry in them; but the prayers that are contained therein are very simple and often refer to the material needs and comforts of the adorers. It is difficult to say whether in the earliest times these Vedic hymns were used as charm verses at different sacrificial performances, or whether they were simply shot forth through the minds of the Vedic poets, embodying their rapturous delights or their simple prayers to Nature-Gods who, they believed, could give them what they wanted. But the practice of sacrifice was probably accepted from very early times in Vedic circles, and these hymns were used, sometimes torn from their contexts and sometimes in their entirety, as having peculiar magical values, in relation to the particular operations of the sacrifices, by virtue of which the adorers could attain their ends when in need of any special favour from the gods to whom the hymns were dedicated. This idea of sacrifice is entirely different from anything found in other races, for to the Vedic people the sacrifices were more powerful than the gods, who might be pleased or displeased, but if the sacrifices were duly performed the prayers were bound to be fulfilled. The utterance and chanting of the stanzas of the Vedic hymns with specially prescribed accents and modulations, the pouring of the melted butter in the prescribed manner into the sacrificial fire, the husking of rice in a particular way, all the thousand details and rituals—often performed continuously for days, months and years with rigorous exactness—formed a Yajña (frequently translated into English "Sacrifice").

2. The introduction of this type of sacrifice gradually weakened the might of the gods who have been extolled in the hymns. It has rightly been pointed out that though a belief in a multitude of gods may naturally be styled polytheism, yet the fact that each god was in turn praised as the ultimate god having the highest powers naturally distinguishes the Vedic religion from the polytheism as ordinarily accepted, and the special name of henotheism has been accorded to it. But if the prayers were fulfilled not by the special favour of the gods but as an unalterable efficacy of the magical operations of the sacrifice, the gods are naturally put into the shade and the sacrifice becomes the most important thing. A belief in the power of the sacrifices performed for the satisfaction of mundane wants and interests cannot be regarded as a high type of religion, and it is curious that this idea of sacrifice assumed such an importance in the minds of the early Vedic people that they could not think of anything else as deserving their attention as the supreme duty than the duty of the study of the Vedas and the performance of sacrifices. The term Dharma, which in later days is used in the sense of righteousness, law, religion, etc., is exclusively used in the Vedic sense as meaning the benefits accrued from sacrifices; the term Karma, which is used in later days in the sense of any kind of deed that is performed, is definitely restricted to the performance of Vedic sacrifices. And no other duty is recognised in the Vedas but the due performance of their injunctions, and these injunctions have almost always a bearing on the performance of sacrifices. The main interest which a student of the history of Indian philosophy may have in this sacrificial culture is the fact that it introduces into the Indian mind a notion that duly performed sacrificial operations must produce the desired results. The substitution of all kinds of deeds for sacrificial ones was an easy thing in the process of time; and the unalterability of efficacy that was associated with sacrificial deeds was thus easily transferred to deeds in general. It is here that we have the beginning of the law of karma. The law of karma is almost universally regarded as an ethical law, by which each person was bound to reap the good and bad effects of his deeds. But it seems to me that the law of karma had its origin in the belief in the magical efficacy of the sacrificial performance, and it was therefore valid by itself before its application in the moral field. It was not because of our moral expectations that a good man should not suffer or that a bad man should not prosper that the law of karma was formulated, but the law of karma was a mere corollary of the belief in the unalterable efficacy of the sacrificial operations to produce good and bad effects. When in later times Indian moral consciousness began to rise to a high eminence, it was not only the sacrificial deeds that were regarded as important; but the great importance of moral and immoral deeds was also universally recognised, and thus the law of karma was expanded along with the expansion of the meaning of karma and it was formulated as a law that controlled the relation of human conduct with human sufferings and enjoyments. The law of karma was thus rooted in the Indian mind from the earliest stages in the trivial belief in the efficacy of magical operations, incantations and the like, and it was only extended at a later stage into the ethical field.

3. But the Rigveda and the Atharvaveda not only contain hymns in the praise of different Nature-Gods, but they also contain at least some hymns where the notion of a universal being seems to have been definitely reached. Thus in Rigveda 129 we have the following verse:

"Then there was neither Aught nor Nought, no air nor sky beyond.
What covered all? Where rested all? In watery gulf profound?
Nor death was then, nor deathlessness, nor change of night and day.
That One breathed calmly, self-sustained; nought else beyond It lay.
Gloom hid in gloom existed first—one sea, eluding view.
That One, a void in chaos wrapt, by inward fervour grew.
Within It first arose desire, the primal germ of mind,
Which nothing with existence links, as sages searching find.
The kindling ray that shot across the dark and drear abyss,—
Was it beneath? or high aloft? What bard can answer this?
There fecundating powers were found, and mighty forces strove,—
A self-supporting mass beneath, and energy above.
Who knows, who ever told, from whence this vast creation rose?
No gods had then been born,—who then can e'er the truth disclose?
Whence sprang this world, and whether framed by hand divine or no,—
Its lord in heaven alone can tell, if even he can show."

Again, the famous *Purusha Sukta* runs as follows:

"Purusha has a thousand heads, a thousand eyes and a thousand feet. On every side enveloping the earth, he transcended it by a space of ten fingers. Purusha himself is this whole, whatever has been and whatever shall be. He is also the lord of immortality, since through food he expands. Such is his greatness; and Purusha is superior to this. All existing things are a quarter of him, and that which is immortal in the sky is three-quarters of him. With three-quarters Purusha mounted upwards. A quarter of him again was produced here below. He then became diffused everywhere among things animate and inanimate, etc."

Again, in Atharvaveda we have another hymn on Skambha and Brahmā, in which it is said:

"Skambha established both these (worlds), earth and sky, the wide atmosphere and the six vast regions; Skambha pervaded this entire universe. Reverence to that greatest Brahmā, who, born from toil and austere fervour (*tapas*), penetrated all the worlds, who made Soma for himself alone. How is it that the wind does not rest? How is not the soul quiescent? Why do not the waters, seeking after truth, ever repose? The great being is absorbed in austere fervour in the midst of the world on the surface of the waters. To him all the gods are joined as the branches around the trunk of a tree. Say, who is that Skambha to whom the gods with hands, feet, voice, ear, eye present continually an unlimited tribute. By him darkness is dispelled; he is free from evil."

Again, the next hymn runs as follows:

"Reverence to that greatest Brahmā, who presides over the past, the future, the universe, and whose alone is the sky. These worlds, the sky and the earth, exist supported by Skambha. Skambha is all this which has soul, which breathes, which winks. That which moves, flies, stands, which has existed breathing, not breathing and winking; that omniform entity has established the earth; that combined is one only....I regard as the greatest That whence the sun rises and That where he sets; he is not surpassed by anything....Knowing that soul calm, undecaying, young, free from disease, immortal, self-sustained, satisfied with the essences, deficient in nothing, the man is not afraid of death."

These and other similar hymns indicate that at least among some persons of the Vedic circle a new intellectual star had dawned. There breathes here a freshness of thought, a bold advance of imagination, an ambitious ideal of going beyond the visible aspects of nature and ordinary mundane interests that is extremely startling. It is almost inexplicable how thought refuses to be shut up within the narrow grooves of desires and their satisfaction, and how the man through its innate inner movement tries to soar above the prejudices, beliefs and limited interests of an immature age. We find here people who shook off the popular beliefs in the supremacy of the Nature-Gods and tried to speculate about the origin of the world, about some master-deity who forged this world into being, who was alone in himself when nothing else existed. It is here probably for the first time in the history of human thought that a thinker hit upon the view that all was God but God was above all, that it was by the spiritual philosophy of His own thought, His own self-contained austerity and self-abnegation that He manifested himself in the glorious diversity of this manifold world, that if there were gods superintending over the diverse parts of nature, there was at least someone who was above them all and He was the creator not only of man and animals but also of the gods. Yet the mystery of this world may yet be inscrutable, for it may be a mystery even to the Lord himself. It is here that we find for the first time the vain spirit of enquiry that wishes to go to the bottom of all things and make a beginning at the very beginning; here is that one penetration of philosophic vision the unsophisticated thinker begins with, a negation—a negation not only of air or sky but also of death and deathlessness, of night and day. Yet this negation could not be merely a negation, and the thought of this was forced in by something that breathed calmly, self-sustained. And it was by the inner fervour of this great being through his will power, the primal germ of mind, spaceless and timeless, with all the mighty forces, that has created the world and helped it to come into being.

It is, therefore, this creation that has ultimately to be traced to the primal deity who stands self-sustained and through whose spiritual fervour everything has come into being, and yet the mystery remains unexplained. I shall not give a long philosophical annotation and interpretation of these hymns; for though they reveal great philosophic insight and wisdom they do not contain that systematic unity and coherence of thought which technical philosophy requires. But yet they undoubtedly tend to show that the philosophic activity of the mind that tries to penetrate deeper and deeper to the foundations of experience is a unique gift of human nature; and that though hemmed in by the crude prejudices of a people who were immersed in ritualistic ideas, the searching mind was not inactive; and it is this searching mind that could not rest contented merely with mundane interests of the concrete facts of nature in their merely concrete bearings on life.

4. It has been said that the "*sine qua non* of magic is a human operator, materials, rites and an aim that borders on the impossible, either in itself such as predicting the future or curing incurable diseases or becoming invisible or in relation to the apparently inadequate means employed".[1] I have attached the term magic to the Vedic rituals in the sense that the Vedic people in general believed in the operations of nature, the condition of human bodies, the efficiency of enemies; as a matter of fact, everything that concerns us in our daily life could be changed, modified or influenced by the performance of sacrifices, provided there were duly qualified priests, the Vedic *mantras* were duly and properly uttered or chanted in their proper accents and the elaborate sacrificial details were performed in strictest accuracy. With the growth of thought and

[1] Thorndike's *A History of Magic and Experimental Science*, vol. II, p. 974.

changes of conditions the idea of sacrifices became so far modified that it was believed that the magical value of the sacrifices could be attained also by particular kinds of meditation, and that in such a case the actual performance of the sacrifices could be dispensed with. It was also believed that deep meditation, self-mortification or asceticism could win for us whatever we wanted. This was, in my opinion, a belief in a new kind of magic, where the performance of mystical operations was replaced by self-centred energy of thought and self-sought sufferings and penances. Thus it was believed that just as a man could attain whatever he wanted by the performance of sacrifices, so he could also achieve his end, however extravagant it might be, by the performance of tapas involving meditation and self-imposed sufferings and mortifications. Thus in the later day Purāṇas we hear many stories of how the gods were forced to give even such boons to the ascetics by which they themselves would come to grief. The story is related how a demon had a boon granted to him by the god Śiva through his own tapas or self-mortification, by which the demon could reduce to ashes anyone on whose head he would rest his palm. The demon wanted to perform the experiment on the god Śiva himself, and the poor god was followed from place to place until by a trick the demon was made to rest his palm on his own head and was thus reduced to ashes. We heard of Viśvāmitra, who though a king was worsted in his quarrel with the priest Vaśiṣṭha who had a magical cow. Desirous of being a Brahmin he performed tapas, but as he was being refused again and again he had the daring plan in his mind of creating a new world in which he could install himself as a Brahmin, and the god Brahmā, being anxious to soothe him, granted him a boon and he became a Brahmin; and the description of the power of tapas goes to show that one could attain the mastery of all the worlds and achieve all impossible things through it. It has also found a place in the scheme of *yoga* practices, which are supposed to be capable of performing miracles by which one could become as small or as large as one wished, may become invisible, fly through the air, or dive into the ground. Thus from the early Vedic times two kinds of magic, viz. that of rituals, and that of tapas, which involved meditation and asceticism, were regarded as being omnipotent, and even the powers of gods were regarded as belonging to a much lower rank. Consistently with this we find that some of the Vedic sages, impelled by the demands of their philosophic nature, could conceive the idea of a great being when nothing else existed and could think of his creating activity as being due either to self-immolation and self-sacrifice or to the fervour of tapas. The idea of this great external being either as Purusha or as Brahmā oscillates between an ill-defined pantheism and monotheism, but it still smacks of the magical elements of sacrifice and tapas which were the prevailing creeds of the time, and even the best minds could not shake them off. It is interesting to note, however, that both the sacrifice and the tapas could at best be regarded as being non-moral. One could perform the sacrifice or the tapas for the most immoral ends and yet one could attain them. We find here the unalterability of the law of karma, where karma stands for sacrifices or tapas; but this law of karma is yet only magical and therefore non-moral and non-ethical. It is only at a later stage that the law of karma becomes formulated as a moral law.

5. In the Prajāpati hymn from Rigveda (10, 121) we read:

> A golden germ arose in the beginning,
> Born he was the one lord of things existing,
> The earth and yonder sky he did establish—
> What god shall we revere with our oblation?

Who gives life's breath and is of strength the giver,
At whose behest all gods do act obedient,
Whose shadow is immortality and likewise death—
What god shall we revere with our oblation?

The king, who as it breathes and as it shuts its eyes,
The world of life alone doth rule with might,
Two-footed creatures and four-footed both controls—
What god shall we revere with our oblation?

Through whose great might arose these snow-capped mountains,
Whose are, they say, the sea and heavenly river,
Whose arms are these directions of the space—
What god shall we revere with our oblation?

Prajāpati, thou art the one—and there's no other—
Who dost encompass all these born entities!
Whate'er we wish while offering thee oblations,
May that be ours! May we be lords of riches!

(Bloomfield's translation.)

Another interesting hymn on Time runs as follows:

"Time carries us forward, a steed, with seven rays, a thousand eyes, undecaying, full of fecundity. On him intelligent sages mount; his wheels are all the worlds. This Time moves on seven wheels; he has seven naves; immortality is his axle. He is at present all these worlds. Time hastens onward, the first god. A full jar is contained in Time. We behold him existing in many forms. He is all these worlds in the future. Time generated the sky and these earths. Set in motion by Time, the past and the future subsist. Time created the earth, by Time the sun burns, through Time all beings exist, through Time the eye sees. Time is lord of all things, he who was the father of Prajāpati. That universe has been set in motion by him, produced by him and is supported on him. Time, becoming divine energy, supports Parameshṭḥi Prajāpati."

6. All these hymns of Prajāpati, Viśvakarmā, Purusha, Time, etc. definitely prove that there were at least some minds among the early Vedic sages who, though they believed in the efficacy of sacrifices and tapas, could yet take a comprehensive view of world-events and could rise to the conception of a mighty creator who holds the universe within himself or from whom the universe has emerged into being; but this god, be he called Prajāpati or Viśvakarmā or Skambha or Brahmā or even Time, is yet external to human nature. It is only a cosmological god who is the fashioner of this universe, the creator of all animate beings, who holds the destinies of us all in his palm, and whom we have to satisfy with our oblations for our temporal well-being. But he is not yet one with our moral nature and he has not revealed himself in our own selves. What may be the nature of this great being? We may call him the highest, the Brahman; but what is this highest, what is this Brahman? It is with this question that the Upanishads opened themselves to us. The narrative is preserved for us in Bṛhadāraṇyaka and Kauṣitki, in which Bālāki-gārgya boasts to King Ajātaśatru that he could explain the nature of this Brahman and he tried in vain to explain this Brahman as the presiding deity of the sun, moon, lightning, ether, wind, fire, water, etc., and in each case the wise king showed him that he was at fault, and the king himself tries to explain the nature of this Brahman through the analogy of deep sleep—how in deep sleep everything is lost and how in the waking stage from this apparently indescribable state we are roused to the consciousness of the world around us. In the Bṛhadāraṇyaka again, Vidagdhaśākalya explains this Brahman as being the highest state of all selves; but in his conversation with Yājñavalkya he is unable to point out the nature of that which is the highest of all selves. In the Chāndogya Upanishad there is a story how five

Brahmins approach Uddālaka Āruṇi with the question regarding the nature of Ātman and Brahman. Uddālaka, being unable to explain, accompanies them to Aśvapati Kaikeya for instruction, and Aśvapati Kaikeya discovers these dreams regarding the ātman and the self as being almost a new kind of god which exists outside of one's self as a supreme divinity. We thus find that the most important question that confronted the Upanishadic sages was the question, "What is self, and what is Brahman (*ko nu ātmā, kiṃ brahma*)?" The Vedic swing of thought which had started with an external Brahman or Purusha had now come back to the self, and the question that occupied the minds of the sages was how to relate the two. It is difficult to see how the notion of self which made itself felt could yet for a long time keep its nature obscure, and how the sages could be perplexed regarding the nature of the self to such an extent as to consider it as an external entity on the same plane as the older Vedic gods. This perplexity is further illustrated in the story in the Chāndogya Upanishad in which Indra and the demon Virocana approach Prajāpati for instruction regarding the nature of the self. Both the gods and the demons found out that it was by knowing the self that one could attain all the benefits of the world and all one's desires, and they, therefore, sent their two deputies, Indra and Virocana, who resided with Prajāpati for 3200 years, and asked him to explain to them the nature of the self. Prajāpati told them that the bodily self, the image of which can be seen in the pupil of the eye or in water or in a mirror, is the immortal self. Putting water in a basin, Prajāpati asked them what they saw in it, and they told him that they saw their bodies finely dressed; and when he said that that was the immortal self, they went away satisfied. But Indra came back and told Prajāpati that the bodily self, the image of which could be seen in a mirror, could not be the immortal self; for this body could be lame or blind or injured, and as such it could not be the immortal self; and Prajāpati then asked him to stay with him for another 3200 years, after which he told him that the self that dreamt in sleep was the ultimate self. Indra went away satisfied, but again returned and told him that the dream-self could not be the ultimate self for it also is affected by bodily defects, by the sufferings and agonies of human life, and as such he was not satisfied that this could be the highest self. Prajāpati asked him to stay again for 3200 years, at the end of which he told him that the true self was a self that was revealed in deep dreamless sleep. It is that which was the highest self which could not be touched by human experiences or affected by bodily defects. Indra raised a further objection that this state would be more like annihilation, and Prajāpati replied that this body was liable to death and decay, and so long as there was any connection with body there would be the painful and pleasurable experiences; it is only when one could go beyond the limits of corporal experience that one could go beyond the limits of good and evil. In deep dreamless sleep, when the distinction of subject and object vanishes, when one does not falsely think oneself to be a man or a woman, or as belonging to a particular race or caste, or as having particular relations with particular individuals, that is, when the so-called light of ordinary conscious experience as subject and object vanishes, it is only then that the highest light of the self reveals itself in its true immortal nature, and it is this light that dawns in deep dreamless sleep. We see here that the true self is neither the body nor the human experiences which are mirrored in dreams. The true self is thus beyond the range of all experience and as such it cannot be explained by any dreams of experience. The same idea is continued in a more advanced manner in the Taittirīya, where five sheaths are described, such as *annamaya*, *prāṇamaya*, *manomaya*, *Vijñānamaya* and *ānandamaya*. The annamaya sheath probably means the inorganic elements of the body, the prāṇamaya means the biological elements which are permeated by the inorganic, the manomaya means the volitional element which is permeated by the biological, the Vijñānamaya is the intellectual or the experiential element and the ānandamaya is the sheath of pure bliss. Thus when a man finds rest and peace in the invisible, unspeakable and the unfathomable, then only he attains his peace.

7. It took, however, a long time before the new enlightenment of the Upanishads could dispel the darkness of the older ritualistic creed; even in the Upanishads we find many instances in which it was believed that the Brahmā should be worshipped or meditated upon as *prāṇa* (the vital organs), as *Vāyu* (air god) or as *manas* and *ākāśa*, and also as other meditative symbols. But these only show how the minds of the Upanishadic sages were gradually emerging from the cloudy atmosphere of ritualistic worship, in which one was being continually suffocated with the demands of desire and their satisfaction through ritualistic means. The search after the highest, which started in certain circles in the domains of the Vedic hymns, was now definitely being directed towards the inner spirituality of man. While the goal of the Vedic people could not go higher than a happy residence in heaven, the Upanishadic sages could not be satisfied with anything less than immortality, and this immortality is not individual survival over infinite time but deathless and indestructible spiritual experience. The story is told in the Kaṭhopanishad, according to which Vājaśravas made a sacrifice involving a gift of all the goods that he possessed. When everything of the sort had been given away, he made a supplementary gift of his cows, which were old and

useless. His son Nachiketas, finding that these gifts would be more embarrassing than useful to the recipients, disapproved of his father's action. He thought that his father had not finished giving his all until he, his son, was also given away. So he asked his father, "To whom are you going to give me?" He was dear to his father, so his father did not like this question and remained silent. But when the question was again and again repeated, the father lost his temper and said, "I give you over to death". Then Nachiketas went to the place of Yama, the king of death, where he remained fasting for three days and nights. Yama, willing to appease him, requested him to take any goods that pleased him. Nachiketas replied that men do not know what happens to people when they pass away from their earthly lives, whether they still continue to exist or whether they cease to exist; and he requested Yama to answer this question on which there are so many divergent opinions. Yama in answer said that this was a very difficult question and that even the gods do not know what becomes of man after he passes away from his earthly life; and that, therefore, he would rather give Nachiketas long life, gold in abundance and whatever else in the way of earthly enjoyment might seem to him desirable. But the philosophical quest was dearer to Nachiketas than all the earthly goods that the king of death could bestow upon him. Money, he thought, cannot satisfy man; money is of use only so long as a man lives, and he can live only so long as death does not take him away. This quest after the ultimate destiny of man and his immortal essence is the best and the highest end that our hearts may pursue. So Nachiketas preferred to solve this mystery and riddle of life rather than to obtain all the riches of the world and all the comforts that they can purchase. The king of death appreciated the wisdom of Nachiketas's choice. He explained that there are two paths leading to two entirely different goals. The mad hankering after riches can only justify itself by binding us with ties of attachment to sense-pleasures which are transitory. It is only the spiritual longing of man after the realisation of his highest, truest and most immortal essence, that does not appeal to people who are always hankering after money. Desire for money blinds our eyes, and we fail to see that there is anything higher than the desire for riches, or that there is anything intrinsically superior to our ordinary mundane life of sense-pleasures and sense-enjoyments. The nature of the highest sphere of life and of the highest spiritual experience cannot be grasped by minds which are always revolving in the whirlpool of mad desire for riches and sense-enjoyments. As the sage in his serene enjoyment of spiritual experience might well think sense-pleasures insipid and valueless, so the people who live a worldly life of ordinary pleasures and enjoyments fail to perceive the existence of this superior plane of life. They think that nothing exists higher and greater than this mundane life of ordinary logical thought and sense-enjoyment. So Yama, the king of death, says to Nachiketas that the majority of the people do not believe there is anything higher than the ordinary mundane life and are content with the common interests of life; that it is only a few who feel the higher call and are happy to respond to it and to pursue a course of life far above the reach of the common man.

8. But what is this undying spiritual essence or existence? Cannot our powers of reasoning, as they are employed in philosophical discussion or logical argument, discover it? If they can do so, then anything which is conceived as loftier than thought and which is considered as the highest principle by which even thought itself and all conscious processes, as well as the functioning of all sense operations, is enlivened and vitalised, cannot be grasped by thought. So Yama tells Nachiketas that this highest spiritual essence cannot be known by any powers of reasoning; only persons who have realised this truth can point this out to us as an experience which is at once self-illuminating and blissful, and it is entirely different from all else that is known to us. Once it is thus exhibited, those who have the highest moral elevation and disinclination towards the earthly enjoyments can grasp it by their inner undivided contact with the reality itself. To Nachiketas's question as to what becomes of man who leaves this earthly life, Yama's answer is that no one is ever born and no one ever dies; birth and death pertain only to our physical bodies, but our consciousness is never born and never dies. The birth and death of the physical body may well be explained with reference to physical causes. The man cannot be identified with his body nor can he be identified with the life which he has in common with all other animals, and even with plants it is the superior truth which vitalises and quickens the process of life, enlivens the activity of thought, and is realised as the very essence of our inner illumination which is also the highest and ultimate principle underlying all common things. He who thinks that he can kill a man, and he who thinks that he may be killed, neither of them knows that the self can never kill nor can be killed. It is subtler than the subtlest and bigger than the biggest, situated in the heart of man. This self cannot be known by too much learning or by a sharp intellect; it can only be known by him to whom the self reveals itself, yet it is beyond all the sense-experiences of colour, touch, sound, taste and smell; it is beginningless, infinite and eternal, and it is only when one knows the true nature of this immortal self that one can become fearless. Death is a dreadful vision for those that regard the sense-experiences of the thought to be the self, but those who know that the true self is beyond them all can never have any mystery of death staring in their faces. Death exists only for the ignorant; for the wise there is only the eternal deathless self.

9. The development of Indian life from the Vedic to the Upanishadic stage marks its transition from a pure unspeculative realism and ritualistic magic for the satisfaction of mundane interests to a form of mystical idealism which not only transcended the bonds of corporal life, the attractions of worldly enjoyments and interests, but also soared beyond the limits of speculative philosophy and merged itself in a mystical experience which is beyond life, beyond mind and beyond thought—unspeakable, unthinkable and unfathomable. The protest against the sacrificial school of thought, which is sometimes observed in the abuses that have been heaped on its followers by such expressions as "It is only the beasts that follow the sacrificial line", may well be understood when one notes the departure of the Upanishadic thought from that of the ritualists. It is important, however, to observe that when the Vedic thought of a mystical ruler and creator of the universe oscillated back to the self of man the enquiry regarding the nature of the self did not reveal to the enquirers a mere subjectivistic thought, a mere *esse est percipi*, for the perceiver admits the existence of things because he perceives them but had found this immortal self beyond all thought. In order to appreciate the real nature of Indian idealism one has, therefore, to disabuse one's mind of the associations that this word has got in European philosophy. It is, therefore, doubtful whether this Upanishadic philosophy should be called idealism or mysticism. It has also given rise to a discussion, In what sense can this type of thought be called philosophy in any technical sense of the word? To one trained in the European schools of philosophy it

becomes difficult to expect any one to go beyond the thought. Yet here we have a philosophy which does not seek to explain the nature of ordinary thought or of life or of physical events or of original knowledge or of any kind of cosmology, but which surrenders itself to the joyous transcendental experience of reality which is beyond all mundane experience—which can be reached only by transcending all thoughts speakable, all thoughts nameable, and all thoughts definable. To the question as to what is the nature of this mystical self, the answer that has been given again and again is that just as a lump of salt when thrown into water loses its form and retains only its taste, so does one who approaches this reality lose himself in it, and then everything he would call his own and everything that he could define and name vanishes, and what is left behind is some transcendent joy, self-complete, self-sustained, self-illuminating and immortal.

Chapter II

UPANISHADIC IDEALISM

1. Professor Sorley, in an article "Two Idealisms" in the *Hibbert Journal*, distinguishes two kinds of idealism. Following Adamson, he says that "the first kind of idealism consists in assigning an existential character to truth and in regarding objects of intellectual apprehension as constituting a realm of existence over against which the world of concrete facts stands in inexplicable opposition". The second type of idealism consists, according to him, in the assertion that reality is spiritual, that all existence has its centre and being in mind. The first kind of idealism seems to be very near to the earlier meanings of idealism as found in Plato. The second type of idealism is, however, what we find to be the special feature of modern idealism, and more particularly contemporary idealism. Contemporary idealism, in spite of the great divergence of views among its exponents, seems to have for its cardinal doctrine the spirituality of the real. But it does not seem that spirituality has the same meaning in all the contemporary forms of idealism. Professor Sorley thinks that it means that all existence has its centre and being in mind, but he does not tell us what he means by mind. What we ordinarily understand by mind has not that precision of meaning which philosophy requires. With us it seems to stand for an entity by means of which all thinking, willing and feeling are possible. What its relation is to these functions of thinking, willing and feeling or the corresponding states has not been made definite and clear by any thinker, and there seems to be little unanimity with regard to the interpretations and

opinions that have been suggested on the point. By spirit we ordinarily mean "self". Do mind and self refer to the same identical (conceptually and numerically) entity? Or is mind some other entity which stands in some separable or inseparable relation to itself? The same question might be asked with regard to the relation between mind and the states, by which term I include the sense-perceptions, images, thought, willing and feeling. Until it is proved that the self or the spirit has the same constituents as the mind or the states, anything which may have the latter for its constituents could not be called spiritual, if the word spiritual means "composed of spirit or spirits". This remark would also apply to any supposition which may regard the spirits as simple entities having no constituent parts. Could we, again, call reality spiritual in a theory which did not believe in the ultimate reality of spirits or self, mind, or any of the states? Could we call any reality which is supposed to transcend the spirits (selves or minds, whatever they may mean) spiritual? Thus Dr McTaggart believes that the universe is composed only of spirits or selves and these have perceptions as their parts; but Mr Bradley thinks that the selves are not ultimately real, but the reality is the whole which contains along with other things the selves as elements. The nature of this whole is that it is Experience, but this experience is very different from all that we ordinarily mean by experience. It does not belong to any person and is neither perception, feeling nor thought, but a reality in which all thinking, feeling and willing have merged and become transfused. Whatever this may be, this is neither spirit nor mind nor anything mental. Berkeley has again often been misrepresented as holding the doctrine of *esse est percipi*, though we know that he believed in two kinds of realities, that of unthinking things *esse est percipi* and that of spirits whose being consisted in the fact that they were percipient. Much of the confusion of Berkeley's system is due to the fact that he could not harmonise these two views upon one single principle or notion of reality. His *Principles of Human Knowledge*, *Hylas and Philonous* and *Siris* reveal to us the three stages of his mental conflict. One who reads the *Principles of Human Knowledge* finds that he does not deny the reality of unthinking things but considers that their nature is *percipi*, whereas one who reads his *Siris* finds that the Universals of Reason overshadow the changing phenomena presented in sense and the suggestions of sensuous imagination. Sensible things are looked at as adumbrations of a reality beyond nature which philosophy helps us to recognise. The objects presented in sense are called phenomena instead of ideas or sensations; while ideas (not in Berkeley's early meaning of the term but in Plato's) are recognised as the supreme objects of meditative thought. This fact has justified to a great extent Kant's criticism of Berkeley in his *Prolegomena*; the dictum of all genuine idealists from the Eleatic school to Bishop Berkeley is contained in this formula: "All cognition through the senses and experiences is nothing but sheer illusion and only in the ideas of the pure understanding and reason there is truth", though what he says in his *Principles* would go directly against any such supposition. Again, Kant calls Descartes a problematic idealist because he denies the independent existence of the external world by treating the *res extensa* as a matter of inference and belief, and thereby placing its reality on a lower level of certainty than that of our internal states. Kant, however, calls his own doctrine "transcendental idealism" on quite different grounds. Thus Kant, in distinguishing other forms of idealism (mainly Berkelean) from his own, says in his *Prolegomena*:

Idealism consists in the assertion that there exist none but thinking entities; the other things we think we perceive in intuition being only presentations of the thinking entity to which no object outside the latter can be found to correspond. I say, on the contrary, things are given as objects discoverable by our senses external to us but of what they may be in themselves we know nothing, we know only their phenomena, i.e. the presentations they produce in us as they affect our senses. I therefore certainly admit that there are objects outside us, that is, things, which although they are wholly unknown to us as to what they may be in themselves, we cognise through presentations, obtained by means of their influence on our sensibility....And just as little as the man, who will not admit colours to be properties of the object itself but only to pertain as modifications to the sense of sight, is on that account called an idealist, so little can my conception be termed idealistic because I find in addition that all properties which make up the intuition of a body belong merely to its appearance. For the existence of a thing which appears is not thereby abolished as with real idealism, but it is only shown that we cannot recognise it as it is in itself through the senses.... What is by me termed idealism does not touch the existence of things (the doubt of the same being what properly constitutes idealism in the opposite sense), for to doubt them has never entered my head, but simply concerns the sensuous presentations of things, to which space and time chiefly belong; and of these and of all phenomena I have only shown that they are neither things (but only modes of presentation), nor determinations belonging to things-in-themselves.

Prolegomena to any future Metaphysics. (How is pure Mathematics possible?)

Again, the idealism as propounded by Hegel, according to most of his non-McTaggartian interpreters, may be regarded as holding that the universe is throughout the work or embodiment of impersonal thought, the course of the development of which is but the self-developing process of thought according to its own inner law, which is a part and parcel of its own nature.

2. If all these different points of view are called idealism, what is the point of agreement between them so that they may be distinguished from other doctrines, say realism? But though it is difficult to define what exactly ought to be the cardinal doctrine of idealism, still it may reasonably be supposed that it is probable that there must be some way in which they may be distinguished, for when we meet with systems of views such as those of Holt or Moore, we agree that they are not systems of idealism. We have seen that the description that idealism is a doctrine which holds that reality is spiritual is not adequate by itself, for the word spiritual has not the same significance in all idealistic systems. But though it may not have the same significance in all idealistic systems, yet it may have a number of such meanings that in none of those senses the reality is regarded as spiritual by non-idealistic systems. If this is possible, then in spite of the internal difference of one idealism from another they may all be distinguished from other systems which are not idealistic. I shall now try to point out some of the important senses in which the descriptive assertion "Reality is spiritual" may be interpreted so as to exclude the non-idealistic systems. The word spiritual may mean pertaining to spirit, self or those states which are most immediately and directly connected with it, viz. perceptions, thoughts, feelings and willing. There may be one impersonal self or a supreme self in which all other selves are contained or by which they are somehow directed, or there may be a number of selves in our ordinary meaning of the term with nothing above them. Perceptions, thoughts, feelings and willing may again be of an individual, of some other supreme self or of an impersonal and absolute nature. Or, again, the word spiritual may mean some such entity which contains the self, thoughts, feelings, etc. as elements only in it, but in itself transcends them all, since by none of these can we get it, but we can get them all in it somehow interfused or welded.

3. The word reality in "Reality is spiritual" may again mean that reality is conceptually and numerically identical with spirituality in any of the above senses, or that it is so connected with it that it is indefinable, incomplete, fragmentary or unknowable without the contributions derived from the latter. I shall call any theory idealistic which asserts that "Reality is spiritual" in any of the above senses of the words spiritual and reality. When a person says that he has refuted idealism he must show that it is an impossible doctrine in any of the above senses. Idealism is not committed to any particular kind of epistemological doctrine. When idealism is therefore defined as a doctrine which asserts that the reality of the external world is its perceptibility, it is an insufficient and unjustifiable assumption. The fault of most of the critics has been that they believed some of the dogmas or some units of idealism to be the cardinal principles of idealism, such that by the refutation of these principles the fundamental principles of idealism are refuted. It may not be out of place to mention that with some notable exceptions most forms of contemporary realism remain at the epistemological stage and do not profess to make any assertion about the nature of metaphysical reality. Thus Holt emphatically points out that the realist asserts: "Things are as they are perceived, not that things really are as they are perceived". The concern of the idealist is with regard to the assertion of the nature of reality, and it is not difficult to conceive that there should be an idealism which is largely in agreement with some forms of realism in the field of epistemology but may yet be thorough-going idealism.

4. In addition to the doctrine that reality is spiritual,

which I believe is held in one sense or other by all true idealists, there is another assertion which I think holds good of most forms of idealism, viz. that our perceptions of the external world cannot give us the assurance that its nature is ultimately such as are revealed by them, i.e. our perceptions are in some sense illusory. This "some sense" is of course somewhat different with different idealists. For even with an idealist like Bosanquet, who agrees to the existence of nature as different from mind, the former does not stand independently by its own right as apart from the mind, as is revealed by ordinary perception, but it is what it is only as a part of the mind-nature whole. An idealist like Dr McTaggart thinks that the sense-data are what we perceive, and that they are not made or manufactured by our minds; but after a long course of logical argument he finds himself driven to a situation in which the only way of avoiding contradiction is found in the assumption that there are only spirits and our perceptions of these sense-data are misperceptions. There seems also to be another proposition which is held by most forms of idealism, viz. that there is an ultimate state of perfection and happiness which exists either as always timelessly accomplished or as being in the course of being accomplished through time. A belief in such an ideal state as the eternally existing absolute or as the ultimate goal of the universal process seems to me to be a fundamental attitude of idealism.

5. Baldwin, in his *Dictionary of Philosophy*, speaking of realism says: "The realist is one who considers that in sense-perception we have assurance of the presence of a reality distinct from the modification of the perceiving mind and existing independently of our perceptions". In spite of great divergence of views among the realists, this characteristic largely holds good of most realists, though the statement has to be differently modified with reference to different realists. But in most cases this statement comes in conflict with the proposition, which I believe holds good of idealism, that our perceptions of the external world are in some sense illusory. The proposition that all our perceptions of the external world are in some sense illusory is a corollary to the proposition that reality is spiritual; for if reality is spiritual the nature of the chairs and tables could not be just as they are perceived.

6. The doctrine that reality is spiritual may therefore be taken as the cardinal principle of idealism. Keeping this principle before our eyes, we may now begin our investigation in Indian philosophy to discover what particular strands of thought may definitely be regarded as idealism. The nature of any particular type of idealism will have to be determined by describing or defining the meaning of the two terms, reality and spiritual, in that particular school of thought. For this purpose I shall ignore other schools of thought which may not be relevant to the subject under discussion. It has been pointed out in the last chapter that philosophical speculations properly began in the Upanishads. Let us, therefore, try to examine the nature of idealistic thought that has found expression in the earlier Upanishads. The Upanishads do not present to us any systematic philosophy in the technical sense. The word philosophy may be used in a variety of senses covering the various elements of thought which are comprised under the name of philosophy. Philosophy may be defined as "the theory of a subject-matter taken as a whole or organised entity containing principles which bind together particular truths and facts and requiring a certain harmony of theory and practice". When I speak of the philosophy of the Upanishads I do not say that the Upanishads present to us a systematic and co-ordinated unity of thought, nor can it be said that they were written by one person at any particular time; they are stray thoughts, which are strung together in particular groups, and their unity is sometimes more artificial than organic. But yet they reflect to us the philosophic culture of a particular circle of people of a particular epoch; that particular type of thought does not rule out the fact that other types of thought were also current in other circles in that age. But though diverse currents of thought may be found to be watering the Upanishadic age, yet the idealistic types are so predominant that it is possible to separate them for review. If we start with the Upanishadic forms of idealism it will be easy for us to trace their growth and change through the succeeding ages. Numerous writers have discussed the philosophy of the Upanishads both in the past and in the present, in this country and even in Europe and America, but the tendency has always been to treat the different Upanishads as being like different chapters of one organically complete work, and various attempts have been made to bring out one synthetic philosophy as a philosophy of the Upanishad. I shall not run into the controversial discussion whether this is possible or not, but as I have limited myself only to the aspects of Upanishadic idealism I shall try to trace the character of this idealism in some of the important Upanishads, taking them separately, and then attempt to generalise on the basis of the views thus gathered.

7. Let us first take the Kena Upanishad. In the first part of this Upanishad it is urged that it is through the driving power of Brahman that our minds, our vital powers, our sensory and motor organs are moved into activity, our eyes cannot reach him or words cannot describe him, our minds cannot know him and he is different from all that is known and unknown and it is therefore impossible to describe his nature. But though our words cannot describe him, yet the power of speech

is derived from him; though our minds cannot know him, yet the power of thought is derived from him; though our eyes cannot see him, yet it is through his vision that the eyes can operate; though our ears cannot hear him, yet it is through him that the organ of the ear can realise itself in hearing. In the second part a story is told that Brahmaṅ was the greatest of the gods. Once the god Agni approached him, asking him who he was, and being asked in his turn Agni replied that he was Agni and that he could burn everything that he wished, and a piece of straw was given him. With all his powers Agni could not burn that piece of straw. When Vāyu, the wind god, approached him and was asked in turn who he was, he said that he was the wind god and that he could blow away the whole world. A piece of straw was offered to him, and with all his powers he could not shake it; and the moral drawn was that the powers of all the Nature-Gods were derived from that of the Brahman and it was through the power of Brahman that everything else appeared as powerful. In discussing the nature of Brahman it is said that he who thinks that he has known him, has not known him, and he who thinks that he has not known him, alone knows him. It is different from all that is known and different from all that is unknown. Yet it is only when Brahman is known that one rests in truth, and so long as one does not know him he is in the realm of destruction.

8. We remember that Brahman appears to us as a god in the Atharvaveda, and there he is described as the greatest being superintending over the past and the future, and Skambha is described as being all that breathe, all that move, fly and stand. It is also said that Brahman was the creator of the gods, that having created the world he pervaded it with name and form and that the gods who were in the beginning mortal became immortal by being pervaded by Brahman. A remnant of

this idea can be traced in the story just told of the intercourse of Brahman with the gods. But in the Vedas, however great the Brahman may be, he remains there only as an external deity, a creator, a ruler of the universe, but he does not appear there as the inner controller of power behind all our sensory and motor powers and our thought. We cannot say in what sense the Brahman who is regarded as the ultimate reality can here be taken as spiritual. It is certain that this spirituality is not intellectual thought, perception or feeling. It is regarded as something from which all our psychical powers are derived and yet it transcends them all. It is at the same time the same power which is the source of all powers that we find in nature, yet it is unspeakable, unthinkable and invisible. To think that one knows it is not to know it; yet it is said that when one knows it one rests in truth. This implies that this reality can only be known through some mystical wisdom. It is undoubtedly nothing that can be called physical and it is also nothing that can be called psychical or intellectual. But since it probably means a being which in some sense is the source of all that we call psychical, though it may transcend them all, it may, therefore, be called spiritual according to the meaning that has been ascribed to the term before. Our only difficulty is that we do not know in what particular meaning this being may be the source of all psychical and physical powers and the Kenopanishad does not make any attempt to describe it. We know also that it is this great being, which is superior to everything else and from which all powers are derived, that is the ultimate truth and that though it cannot be cognised either by the senses or by the logical powers of thought it can yet be somehow grasped or realised. The fact that the ultimate reality cannot be attained by reason or by the senses, and that it may yet be grasped or realised in some other ways, reduces this conception of Brahman into a form of mysticism. The reality is neither subjective nor objective, but is such that both the subject and the object derive their very existence from it. It may, therefore, be regarded as a sort of mystical idealistic absolutism.

9. In the Kaṭhopanishad this reality is described as invisible, all-pervading, yet hidden deep in the cave, which could only be realised through the spiritual touch, and by whose realisation all emotions of sorrow and pleasure disappeared. It remains hidden in all individuals and can only be realised by the sharp wisdom of an unwavering mind. It is beyond all sensations of sound, touch, colour, taste and smell; it is beginningless and infinite. It is the inner essence of man, which is never born and ever eternal, which suffers no change with the destruction of the body; in one sense it is the subtlest of the subtle, in another sense it is the greatest of the great; it lies hidden in all beings and it is only when a man is discharged of his passions that he can perceive it as the very greatness of his own soul. It has no body and with all changes of body it remains unchanged. It cannot be known by much learning, scholarship or sharp intellect; it can only be known by him to whom it reveals itself. It is neither virtue nor vice, neither cause nor effect, neither past nor future; yet it is the goal of all the Vedas and all religious fervour. It is by realising this that one saves oneself from death.

10. Any man can see through his senses, but it is only when he turns away from the senses that he perceives it. All our sense-enjoyments and sense-expressions are possible because of its existence and there is nothing that remains beyond it. Both our waking and dream experiences are cognised, as it were, by it; it is the great self of ours. Whatever we find in the world has its essence in this reality and it is this reality which has pervaded all that we see, and he who cannot establish him-

self in this unity and only perceives "the many" of the world is doomed to destruction. It is to be grasped by one's mind as the one unchangeable entity and there is nothing around us that can be called "the many". Just as after a shower on the hill the waters that had deluged it rush downwards, so do all phenomenal appearances flow away leaving this unchangeable reality in its unshakable unity. When the body decays and ceases to exist, what remains there, what abides? It is not by the vital process of life that the man lives, but it is through the other in which all vital processes show themselves that the man lives. It is the permanent and immortal essence in man which enlivens the vital processes into life, and it is this essence that lives in man and builds his experiences both in the waking stage and in sleep. It is this in which all the worlds are supported, which nothing else can transcend; it is the Brahman, the immortal. Just as one element of light manifests itself in diverse colours in this world, so does this one being who abides as an inner essence of all manifest itself in all outward forms; just as the one sun remains untouched by all the defects of the eyes of those who perceive it, so it also remains untouched by the sorrows and afflictions of all beings. It remains in itself as one self-controlled, self-centred entity, and yet it manifests itself in diverse forms as the universal principle of all beings, and those only that can perceive it within their own selves can attain the real bliss. It is the one eternal among all transient things, one conscious principle amongst all living beings. It is indefinable, for there is no way of cognising it through ordinary means. No sun sheds its light on it, no moon, no stars; the lightning and the fire lose all their shiny character before it, because it is through the light of this great illumination that everything else derives its light. The whole world, the sun, the fire, the wind, the lightning, and even death follow their own courses through fear of this great being. No one can see it with one's eyes, it is only the wise and the saintly that can grasp it in their hearts and become immortal. It is only when all the cognitive elements and thought processes are suspended and arrested, all the powers of reasoning are paralysed, that the spiritual touch by which it can be realised is attained. No one can describe it by words or conceive it in imaginations; for of it nothing can be said than that it is the pure being. This reality is only realised as a mere be-ness, for all characters, all qualities, all descriptions are outside of it, and when all the knots of the heart that tie us to worldly things are torn asunder, this great truth and this great reality can be realised as the one inmost self that abides in us all, separate from the body, separate from all our living organs, separate from our minds and thought, separate from all that we can conceive of.

11. When we review before our mind the above ideas of the Kaṭhopanishad we find that the remnants of the older idea of Brahman as an external god had not ceased. It is this god who is compared with a aśvattha tree which has its roots high up in the transcendent region and its branches forming our world beneath, and thus its sphere with the entire external order of things is maintained in its proper place; but yet this idea of an external god has been very largely thrown into the shade by the more dominant idea of a reality which is regarded as forming the mysterious essence of the inner selves of all beings; and it is this essence which is regarded as having manifested itself in all the outward forms and nature of the manifold world around us. It is this reality which is regarded as the ground and support not only of all our waking and dream experiences but also of all the vital functions, powers and capacities that form our psychical will. It has again and again been pointed out that it is this inner reality that is the absolute

and ultimate truth, all other characters and forms that strike our senses and which form "the many" of the world are in a way delusive, and any emphasis that we may give to this side of "the many" is bound to lead us to destruction. The way to immortality, then, is to turn our spiritual eye to the true ultimate reality of our indestructible innermost essence. This innermost essence cannot be any further defined or described, for it has no other character than that of pure being. All other characters are external to it and slip over it like waters from a hill-top, which cannot be known by any ordinary known means of cognition, and it can only be grasped or realised through communion. Death or mortality, therefore, belongs only to the body or the other psychical elements of ours which are associated with the body and not with this innermost essence, which is untouched by all our senses and all our intellectual powers and is therefore naturally beyond any change; but though this innermost essence is beyond the range of our senses and cognitional modes and all that we perceive around us in the external world, yet they can function in their proper spheres only because they are grounded in it as their ultimate reality. Reality here is thus not mental but spiritual, in the sense that it admits spiritual essence, which is regarded as the ground of all that we call mind or mental and all that we call matter or material. The mysticism of this idealism is evident when we remember that the Kaṭhopanishad does not attempt to describe or define the nature of this spiritual essence which is in a way unknowable, and unrealisable by the senses and all characters stand outside of it; it can only be described as "being". It is regarded as residing in a deep cavern of the heart (*guhāhitaṃgahvareṣṭpam*) and no further light can be shed on it. But how this inmost essence can be the ground of support of all our psychical nature, functions and experiences, and how remaining unchanged in itself it can manifest itself in all the diverse forms and characters of the external world, remains a mystery, and the Kaṭhopanishad does not give us any answer. It seems pretty certain that the inmost essence of reality, which is so strongly emphasised in the Kaṭha Upanishad, was grasped by its seers, not philosophically but mystically, and the links of arguments which a philosopher may be anxious to discover are fortunately or unfortunately almost entirely missing.

12. Let us now turn to the Praśna Upanishad. An individual person or a psychical or psychological entity is here described as being composed of sixteen parts, such as the vital form or prāṇa, the five material elements, deeds, faith, energy, fervour, mind, names, etc., but they are all grounded in the inmost essence that resides in us, and all the different components of an individual are derived from it; just as all rivers that flow into the sea lose their names and forms in it, so do all the parts of the individual return to the inmost essence and lose themselves entirely in it. In another passage it is said that an individual is composed of the grosser and subtler parts of the elements; the sensibles, the sense-faculties, the motor-faculties and their objects, mind and the thinkable, will and that which is willed, memory and that which is remembered, the vital powers and those which are upheld by them, all these combined form a person who sees, touches, hears, smells, tastes, thinks, wills, works and understands, and just as birds rest themselves in their residing tree, so the entire person with all these component factors is ultimately grounded in the indestructible self (*ātman*).

13. The special point of view of the Praśna Upanishad consists in the fact that it tries to elaborate the nature of a psychological person with its psychological components—an idea which may have inspired the theory of composition of personality in Buddhism. This enquiry is almost wholly concentrated on the problem of the psychological individual and its experiences, and in trying to discover the ultimate support of this psychological individual in all its waking and dream experiences, consisting of its faculties, thoughts, senses and their objects, it asserts that the highest self is not only the ground and support of it but that all psychological individuals ultimately lose all their individuality and specific characters when they merge themselves in this higher self, like waters of a river in the ocean. The point of departure of this Upanishad from others that have already been treated lies in the fact that its reflections are limited to the psycho-biological self. It tries to analyse the psycho-biological into its component parts, and says that they are ultimately to be regarded as the manifestations of the highest self; but regarding the nature of the highest self it is unfortunately silent, and we are not in a position to say whether this higher self is to be regarded as the inner essence of man as in the Kaṭhopanishad, or whether it is to be regarded as a superior non-subjective spiritual entity.

14. The Muṇḍaka Upanishad opens with a dialogue between Śaunaka and Āṅgirasa in which Śaunaka approaches Āṅgirasa and asks him "What being known all else becomes known", and Āṅgirasa replies that there are two Sciences, the superior and the inferior. The inferior learning consists of the study of the Vedas and their accessory literatures, such as grammar, lexicon, etc.; the superior science is that by which one realises the indestructible—that which is uncognisable by the senses of the mind, ungraspable by the motor powers, that which has no colour, no ears, no eyes, no hands and feet, that which is eternal, all-pervading, subtle, unchangeable, the cause of all being, having no cause of itself and which is realised by the seers. Just as a spider weaves out its threads from itself and extends them out, just as a plant grows from earth, just as a hair grows from the body of a man, so has this entire universe come out of this indestructible reality. This Brahman works through the powers of its omnipotent thoughts and it is this thought—activity that forms its fervour as tapas by which the world—all its names and forms—has been created. Pursuing another simile, it says that just as thousands of sparks start from the flaming fire, so do all diverse kinds of beings come into being from this reality. This immortal Brahman is described as being in front of us, behind us, on the right of us, high above us and down below us, so that it has spread itself throughout the world and all that we see is but this great reality. The earth, the sky, the moon and the vital organs are ultimately grounded in it and it is this that has to be regarded as the only real self, everything else is but mere words. The Muṇḍaka says that there are two selves, the lower and the higher, and it is the former that enjoys all the experiences, whereas the higher remains all through as the unperturbed seer, and it is only when this lower self can perceive the higher self as its lord that it becomes free from all passions; when it perceives this great self as the cause of all, as the ultimate creator of the world, then it loses all its sins and virtues and, becoming pure, it becomes like it (higher self). This self is the resplendent power, the pure white light inside us, and can only be attained by truth, by fervour, right knowledge and self-control. It is great, self-illuminating, unthinkable and subtle. It is farther than the farthest and yet hidden in the cavern of the heart of the seers who perceive it. It cannot be perceived by the eyes nor described by words nor attained by the worship of gods, asceticism or sacrificial deeds, but can only be realised through meditation, through the illumination of wisdom. It cannot be attained by those who are weak nor by religious fervour and self-renunciation. Just as all rivers flow into the ocean and lose their names and forms, so does the seer lose his name and form, when he becomes free, when he loses himself in the true freedom of this great truth. He who knows Brahman becomes himself Brahman, and being freed from the knots of passions and sorrows passes away from the regions of passions and senses and becomes immortal. It is this knowledge of the immortal Brahman that is the true and superior knowledge. The path of sacrifice is feeble, and those who follow it follow the path of decay, old age and death. Those who are led by sacrificial advisers to follow this course of sacrifice are like blind men led by other blind men. It is only the fools who remain satisfied in performing the sacrifices. The true path is the path of knowledge and self-control by which the Brahman, the highest reality, can be reached.

15. We have seen that in the Kenopanishad it is said that all the powers of the Nature-Gods and all the powers of our inner faculties are derived from Brahman. We have seen in the Kaṭhopanishad that just as one light appears in diverse colours, just as one air appears in diverse aerial forms, so does one Brahman appear throughout the universe in diverse forms. We have also seen that the order of external reality is set up and kept in its proper place through fear of Brahman, but nowhere has the creation of the world from Brahman been so definitely emphasised as in the Muṇḍaka Upanishad; yet this creation is different from the creation of the world by the Brahman as an external creator, as in the Atharvaveda, and some remnants of it have been traced both in the Kena and in the Kaṭha Upanishads. Here in the Muṇḍaka Upanishad four similes have been given of the creation of the world from Brahman. One is that of the spider producing its own threads out of its body and extending them outside; the other is that of plants growing out of the earth; the other that of the hair growing out of human bodies; and the last one, the sparks coming out of fire. In all these similes we are reminded of the fact that the effect in all these cases is but a modification or transformation of the cause, and it does not seem improper to think that according to Muṇḍaka the world has come into being or emerged into existence as a natural transformation from the nature of Brahman; Brahman does not indeed exhaust himself in the world, and the world has simply sprung out of Brahman as a natural emanation. Therefore it is said that since the emanation has the same nature as that of Brahman, the Brahman is in front of us, behind us and on all sides of us. This Brahman, however, is not regarded as an external deity but as a spiritual light revealing itself through the mystical wisdom of the seers. The side of the creation of the world from Brahman is as much emphasised as the side of the spirituality of Brahman as the inner essence of man. Distinction is made between the man as a person, the enjoyer of experiences, and his higher self as beyond all experiences; yet this lower self of man is to be shot through the higher self as its target, by which means the arrow is lost in the target. On the one hand the Brahman is described as omniscient and omnipotent; on the other he is described as the self that resides in the heart of man. It is the biggest of the big, as the whole universe is but an emanation from it, and yet it is the subtlest of the subtle, as it lies hidden in the cave of the heart. The universe being an emanation from Brahman and Brahman being the inmost spirit of man, the spiritual nature of the world is evidently established, but the question remains unsolved, In what sense can the world be regarded as an emanation from Brahman when Brahman is considered as the inner spiritual illumination in man? How can the physical world with its material forms and laws be regarded as an emanation from the spiritual illumination that forms the inmost self in man? To such a question we find no answer in the Muṇḍaka Upanishad. Indeed one of the most important difficulties in dealing with the Upanishadic idealism consists in the fact that no interpretation is given as to how and in what sense the mystical, spiritual nature of man can be regarded as the cause from which the universe is produced. In what sense, again, this mystical spiritual entity can be called omniscient or omnipotent is a question which has found no further answer in the Muṇḍaka than that it can be realised by the seer when he ceases to encourage all mundane desires, when he takes to religious fervour and renounces all things, and that this attainment can only be through the mystical illumination and meditation of Brahman as the one unchangeable and partless being. It is then that the fifteen parts which form the composite man vanish, and all his deeds and knowledge also vanish in the ultimate unchangeable unity of the supreme self. The seer is lost in Brahman as a river is lost in the ocean. The interpretations that have been given of Upanishadic idealism as a whole will be taken up in the later chapters. One way, however, of reconciling the difficulty may be by regarding the Brahman as a great reality and a great being who has two diverse kinds of manifestations, the one as the physical world outside and the other as the inner psychical nature of man. But both these forms are but emanations from his being and do not represent his essential nature, which can only be discovered and realised by the destruction of all desires and by the dawn of spiritual illumination. The reality, however, which is grasped or realised by this spiritual illumination is bound necessarily to be mystical, as it cannot be expressed either in terms of thought in general, or in terms of any physical entity. Viewed in this light, thought and materiality would be like two attributes of Brahman, and in that way the Muṇḍaka may be supposed to be enunciating a philosophy which is akin to that of Spinoza.

16. Māṇḍūkya is a small Upanishad which says that the self as Brahman has four stages: the first, the waking stage in which external objects are known; the second, the dream stage where one ignores experiences, the ideas already acquired; the third, the stage of dreamless sleep in which no dreams are seen, no desires are active, which is regarded as one flow of consciousness which does not manifest itself in any forms, and it is said that it is this self that reveals itself at this stage that is the lord of all, the cause of all origin and destruction, and the inner controller within us. There is a fourth ātman which is regarded as having none of the characteristics of the above three stages, which is invisible, ungraspable, undefinable, unthinkable, which has no pragmatic use, wherein all appearances have ceased, and which remains identical in itself as the one. The mysticism of this little Upanishad has been brilliantly elaborated and interpreted by Gauḍapāda and it will be taken up in a later chapter. Without anticipating what I shall say in that chapter, I can only point out that the reference to the fourth self, which is not described as pure consciousness or bliss and which is supposed to transcend even mystical experience that is felt in dreamless sleep and which is regarded as in every way a negation, and without any name or distinction of any kind, marks a new stage in the development of Upanishadic idealism which has not been treated elsewhere in the Upanishads with so much force. Thus the ultimate reality is described as unperceived, unrelated to experience, unknowable, unthinkable, unnameable, indefinable—the quintessence of all world-appearances, which is the one in which everything else has ceased, and it is this that is

the ātman. The language of such description reminds one of Nāgārjuna's negative description of the ultimate truth, only with this difference that here the stuff or entity or whatever it may be so described is called ātman.

17. The chief importance of the Taittirīya Upanishad lies in the emphasis that it gives on the nature of Brahman as pure bliss which is unthinkable by the mind and unutterable by speech, and when this is once realised all fears cease. According to this Upanishad the world has proceeded out of bliss and people are living through bliss and ultimately enter into this bliss. It further says that there was nothing in the beginning, and that the Brahman wishing to be many through its fervour of tapas created all that we see, definable and the undefinable, truth and falsehood, and ultimately enters into them all himself. So everything which is being and which is non-being is all supported in Brahman as the ultimate reality, and it is through the fear of this Brahman that the wind blows, the sun rises, the fire god, the Indra and death, are all running their proper course. In describing the composition of human personality it divides it into five sheaths, of which the last is the sheath of pure bliss, by which the man completes himself. There is not much to discuss in this Upanishad. It sometimes lapses back even into the older form of theism, when it says that the various parts of nature perform their regular duties only through the fear of Brahman, and where Brahman is regarded as an external being who created the world by tapas. But in spite of this it (Brahman) has thoroughly permeated through it, and this is evidenced by the fact that it takes blissfulness as the innermost of the most ultimate sheath that constitutes the personality of man and identifies Brahman with bliss (*ānanda*). It is absolutely silent as to how the world could spring out of pure bliss or how it was possible for Brahman to create the conscious and the unconscious, and all that we see, by his tapas. The whole concept of creation through tapas seems to me to be pre-Upanishadic. The same idea occurred in the Muṇḍaka also, but there tapas is definitely taken in the sense of thought and it is said that the tapas of Brahman is thought activity. That, however, could not make the interpretation of the origin of the world from Brahman easier, inasmuch as the world seems to have been always regarded even in that Upanishad as materialistic; and the Brahman himself being beyond thought, it is difficult to understand how he could take thought activity as a means for the production of the universe.

18. Turning to the Chāndogya Upanishad, we find that it says that everything that we find around us is Brahman, everything is produced out of it and everything returns back to this Brahman, and this Brahman is the self which is the subtlest of the subtle, dwelling in the inside of the heart, and it is that which is bigger than the world, bigger than the sky and bigger than the entire universe, which is the source of all our deeds, desires, sensations and experiences. Referring to this subtle spiritual essence Āruṇi says to his son Śvetaketu, "It is this subtle essence, which is identical with the universe, the ultimate reality, and thou art that essence, Oh Śvetaketu". Taking the example of a big tree, Āruṇi says that if any one strikes it with a weapon and cuts down a branch it will dry up; if a second branch is cut that also dries up; when any part of it is dissociated from life it dies but the life itself never dies; it is the subtle essence and it alone is ultimately real and this is the self and that art thou, Oh Śvetaketu. Taking a seed of a fine banyan tree, Āruṇi asks his son to split it up into parts and also asks him, "What do you find in it?" He said, "I do not find anything inside it". Then he spoke to him, "Though you do not find anything in this fine seed yet it is out of this subtle essence that the big banyan tree grows. Believe, therefore, that the entire universe and the ultimate reality is nothing but the subtle essence which is the highest self". Throwing a lump of salt in the water he asks his son, Śvetaketu, to see him again in the morning, and when he comes in the morning he asks him to "Get the salt that you threw in this water last night out of it", and Śvetaketu said that he did not know how to do it. Āruṇi told him, "Just as you cannot perceive the salt with your eyes, yet you can perceive it by tasting the water, so the ultimate reality also exists just the same though it cannot be perceived by the senses. And this ultimate reality, the fine essence, is thus the entire universe, and that again is nothing but the highest self". So here also we find the old teaching strongly emphasised that the ultimate reality is the subtle spiritual essence of man.

19. One of the most important contributions of the Chāndogya Upanishad consists in the way in which it tries to enunciate the relation of cause and effect. In the Muṇḍaka Upanishad the question was asked: "What is that which being known everything else would be known?" No direct answer is given to that question there, but Āṅgirasa in answer to this question describes in some detail the nature of the "superior science" by which the ultimate reality can be known. The same question is repeated in Chāndogya, where Āruṇi asks his scholarly son Śvetaketu if he can tell him of anything which being known everything else would be known, and on his failing to reply his father enunciates the doctrine of causation which is regarded as the most important discourse on the subject. He says that when a lump of earth is known, all that is earthen is known, when a piece of iron is known, all that is made up of iron is also known by that fact; for what is true of all earthen wares or of iron things is but the earth and the iron, that alone is true and all the rest is mere name and form. We have again and again heard the doctrine repeated that Brahman alone is what is ultimately real. We have also heard that the entire universe has come out of this Brahman, and we now hear a view which seeks to explain in what sense the Brahman is to be regarded as what alone is ultimately real. For if everything else is but a transformation of Brahman, then since all the effects cannot be regarded as having any further determinable reality than the stuff out of which they are made, they are to be regarded as but mere modifications having particular forms and names, and the only reality that can be attributed to them applies to the material stuff. So, if the whole universe is to be viewed as being only a transformation of the nature of Brahman, the ultimate reality can only be affirmed of the substance of transformation, the Brahman. We had before this a number of passages in which the Brahman is identified with the subtle essence, which is the same as the self of man, and though it is not possible to point out any mode of operation by which this subtle essence of a man could be transformed into the universe, yet we are asked to believe that it is so. The view of the relation of the universe with Brahman that is here formulated in the Chāndogya Upanishad is entirely different from the view expressed in the Muṇḍaka Upanishad, for there the universe is looked upon as being in some way a real transformation (*pariṇāma*) from the nature of Brahman as opposed to the *Vivarta* view in Chāndogya, where the material cause is the only reality and the transformations are mere illusory forms. In the Muṇḍaka the Brahman as such transcends the emanations that arise out of him. The emanations, however, so far as can be judged from the similes, are regarded as real evolutionary products from his nature.

20. In the Bṛhadāraṇyaka it is said that the Brahman has two forms: that which is visible and that which is invisible, and we know that it is said in the Taittirīya that Brahman is both conscious and that which has no consciousness. So the view that it is the Brahman that constitutes the entire reality finds its expression in the Brihadāraṇyaka as elsewhere, and the most notable contribution in the Brihadāraṇyaka Upanishad consists in the emphasis that it gives to the fact that the self is the dearest of all dear things. Thus it says that the innermost self is dearer than the son, dearer than riches, dearer than everything else, and it is only by regarding the self as the dearest that one can attain the true bliss. The same idea is repeated in the well-known dialogue between Maitreyī and Yājñavalkya, where Maitreyī says to her husband that she did not want anything by which she could not be immortal, and Yājñavalkya in an eloquent speech explains to her that everything is true to us because the self is true to us and that it is this self that has to be meditated upon and realised; that by the realisation of this self everything else becomes known. All the caste differences and all other kinds of diversities are based upon a false notion of "difference" (*bheda*), for in reality there is nothing else but the self. What we perceive around us is this self. Just as a lump of salt when thrown in water loses itself in it and it cannot be separated out of it, and in whatsoever part the water is tasted it appears as saline, so is this infinite universal consciousness, and all the diverse forms and names that arise out of the universe around us are ultimately merged and lost in it. None of their specifications, individualities or separate existences can be further differentiated in this ultimate reality. It is only in the region of duality that there is the perceiver and the perceived, the hearer and that which is heard, the thinker and the object of thought, the knower and the known. The ultimate reality being the self of all, who is there to smell anything, who is there to perceive anything, who is there to hear anything, who is there to know anything, who is there to think anything, how can the ultimate perceiver which is the essence of all be perceived by anything else? This self is further described in another passage, where it is identified with the experience of dreamless sleep as beyond all desires of sins and of fear; it is a blissful experience through which one forgets all else that one knows, and it is the essence in which all the normal relations of father, mother, gods, ascetics, sinners and worldly man cease, which is beyond sin and virtue, wherein the heart transcends the realm of all sorrows. No one can perceive this self, for there is no perceiver when it is perceived, because the pure perceiving illumination of this supreme essence never ceases to shed its eternal light. All the senses of the man cease to operate here, but yet the underlying consciousness of all knowledge remains just the same. All ordinary cognitions are bound to be unavailing here, for they all imply impurity of contents; but yet as it is the underlying ground of all knowledge, sensible or mental, its own illumination shines forth its pure effulgence without any change, any impurity or any limitation. It is only by the realisation of this reality that we exist, and it is through its ignorance that we die. It is this realisation that is true immortality. Being in the heart, unborn and undecaying, it is at the same time the lord of the universe; it cannot be touched by good or bad deeds and it is this which is the goal of all true seekers; it is for this that people renounce the world, and yet it can only be pointed out merely by the negative process that it is not anything that one can speak of. It is the great self of man, the Brahman, and he who knows Brahman becomes Brahman.

21. But though we find here that all the multiplicity of this manifold world is positively changed and the inner self of man is regarded as the ultimate reality, yet there is a certain passage in the Bṛhadāraṇyaka where the view of the reality of the world is in a way admitted, and it is held that the inner self of man is the inner controller which abides in the earth and controls it though the earth does not know it, which residing in the water controls it from the inside though the water does not know it, which residing in the fire controls it from inside though the fire does not know it, which remaining in the sun controls it from within though the sun does not know it, which remaining in the moon and the stars controls them though they do not know it, which remaining in all beings controls them from within, which remaining in the eye controls the eye, remaining in the ear controls the ear, remaining in the mind controls the mind, remaining in thought controls the thought, though none of them may know it as its ultimate controller. It is the eternal indwelling, immortal controller; it is the invisible seer, the unheard hearer, the unthought thinker, and there is nothing else beyond it—the thinker, knower and the perceiver.

22. The most important point in the Upanishadic idealism that has been brought forth in great clearness in the Bṛhadāraṇyaka Upanishad is the doctrine that the inmost self is of the nature of pure consciousness, which is the ground of all our experiences and which is at the same time the inner controller of all the diverse powers of nature and in the living bodies, which cannot, however, have any further independent reality from it. It has again and again been emphasised that everything else is dear to us because the self is dear to us, yet this dearness of self to us does not imply any duality, for it is itself regarded as the nature of pure bliss. All the bliss of beings that can be found in the world around us and in all our experiences is possible only because they are all grounded in this ultimate bliss, the self, as their ultimate cause or reality.

23. We have made a brief survey of all the central doctrines of the principal Upanishads, and we are satisfied that the dominant spirit of these Upanishads reveals an idealism in which all reality is ascribed to the spirit as the ultimate inner essence of man, which is different from what we ordinarily understand by soul, the five senses, and the vital powers of the mind. We have found that in some of the Upanishads the idea of an external Brahman or lord as controlling the universe and also the inner functions of man, has been introduced; but in others this Brahman is definitely pronounced to be the inner essence of man; until we come to the Brihadāraṇyaka the nature of this inner essence of man remains very largely a mystery, and though in some of the other Upanishads the idea may lie scattered here and there, it is in the Bṛhadāraṇyaka that the view that this inmost self is of the nature of a pure perceiving consciousness is very definitely emphasised. No attempt is made anywhere in the Upanishads to show how from this one reality of a pure perceiving consciousness the diverse experiences which make up our psychological being can be explained; we are however sometimes told that this universe is only Brahman, or that this universe has sprung out of Brahman and would return back to it, or that this universe is a transformation or manifestation of the nature of Brahman, or that this universe has for its inner controller the Brahman who is of the nature of our inmost self, no attempt is made to explain by what operation the inmost self of man can be regarded as the source or cause of this manifold world. In understanding the nature of the self we are gradually pushed to a mystical conception of it, which is so subtle as to transcend the realms of thought; it cannot be grasped by the senses or by the cognitional modes of our experiences, it can only be realised through self-control, the cessation of all desires,

and the meditation of the spiritual reality. In some cases the Upanishadic sages anticipated our difficulty of understanding how this subtle mystical essence could be regarded as the cause of this visible, apparently material and ponderable universe. Many illustrations are offered to make us believe that it is so still. It does not seem that the Upanishads actually deny the reality of the visible world, but they urge that the ultimate reality underlying it is Brahman or the mystical self within us. But how the "many" of the world can arise out of one, the self, and in what sense the reality of the world can be regarded as spiritually grounded, remains a question which has never been explained in the Upanishads. The sages of the Upanishads liberated Indian thought from the grasp of the ritualistic thinkers and also from purely deistic or theistic concepts. The whole atmosphere of the Upanishads seems to be ringing with the mystical music, and the sages were almost intoxicated with their discovery of the highest reality or the inmost self of man, that whatever we perceive around us is Brahman, that all our thoughts, all our beings, all our experiences are grounded in it, and that in spite of apparent diversities there is the one ultimate reality in which both the microcosm and the macrocosm are united.

Chapter III

UPANISHADIC IDEALISM (*continued*)

1. In the Upanishads two principles have been admitted as the ultimate reality, the Brahman and the mystical innermost self, and in various passages these two principles have been identified as referring to the same reality. From the general tone of the Upanishads it is difficult to discover what exactly is the status of reality that is ascribed to the external world and to the psychical or psychological self, the possessor of all experiences and the knower of the external world. There are some passages in which it is said that the pluralistic view of the world leads to death, whereas the monistic view of the world leads to immortality; and in many passages it is said that the ultimate reality underlying the world and our psychological experiences is the Brahman or the innermost self. But it seems difficult to suppose from this that the world as such was regarded as absolutely false. The more proper view seems to be that only a lesser kind of reality was ascribed to the world and the psychological self, and the denial of the "many" was probably due to an exclusive emphasis that was given to this underlying reality. On the one hand it was due to the enthusiasm of the new discovery of one fundamental spiritual essence as being the ground of the world, and on the other hand it was probably due to a protest that was felt against the ritualists, whose religion was based entirely on the view of a pluralistic world. Under the circumstances it is difficult to label the Upanishadic idealism either as subjective idealism or as objective idealism or as absolute idealism. These terms occur in European philosophy, and they refer to particular systems of thought. Thus, for example, Fichte's philo-

sophy is universally acknowledged as being that of subjective idealism, because he derived the world from the Ego; but this Ego in Fichte is not the subjective individual; it is the universal ego transcending the limits of the psychological subjective self. This Ego is a sort of pure reason, which for the higher need of the realisation of its own supreme ideal, out of its own necessity, posits both itself and the non-ego, and has out of their synthesis produced the so-called external world as the sphere within which it can strive to realise its own end. If new interpretative elements are not introduced into the Upanishads it would be difficult to call the Upanishadic idealism subjective idealism after the analogy of Fichte, for no passage in the Upanishads seems to indicate that the self out of its own practical necessity deduced the world through a process of self-position, as being the only way in which it could realise itself. The only passages that (seem to) refer to the doctrine of self-creation seem to be those in which it is said that the one existent being wanted to be many and so created the world out of itself. But this does not indicate the method by which the process of the derivation of the world as a mode of self-deduction can be explained. The philosophy of Schelling is regarded as a standard form of objective idealism; nature is not expressed as being merely an opposition or obstacle as non-ego which has to be overcome, but it is regarded as visible intelligence, and intelligence is regarded as invisible nature. In Schelling's system nature is the ego or the self in process of becoming. Nature is developing itself through its own categories with a particular end in view, and it "is ruled by the thought that even in the objective, reason struggles always from its material modes of manifestation through the multitude of forms and transformations of force, up to the organism in which it comes to consciousness".

2. It is clear that in the Upanishads we do not find many passages which can force upon us a view that the Brahman can be regarded as an objective intelligence, which has developed itself through the diverse forms of the manifold world until it attains the status of conscious intelligence in man. In Hegel we find the view that the real or actual is the manifestation of spirit or mind, which determines itself according to the notion or logic that is involved in its own nature, but this spirit cannot be directly intuited or immediately perceived. The process of the evolution of the manifestation of this spirit in subjective and objective forms and categories is more or less an illusion, for the spirit is eternally realised in itself. Nature is like "petrified intelligence", and in history we realise the necessary stages of the development of the spirit towards self-realisation. Nature is therefore to be regarded as rational in all its multiplicity. What is rational is real and what is real is rational; but though the task of philosophy is thus to be understood as a comprehension of the evolution of this real as reason through its dialectic forms, yet since all forms of the real are comprehended in reason, and since all dialectic varieties that take part in evolutionary forms are comprehended in the nature of reason, the reason is in itself self-complete. "The consummation of the infinite end consists merely in removing the illusion which makes it still unaccomplished. In the course of its process the idea makes itself that illusion by supplying an antithesis to confront itself, and it again consists in getting rid of the illusion which it has created" (Wallace's *Logic of Hegel*). The fundamental difference of such a view from that of the Upanishads seems to be that the Upanishadic spirit can be realised through mystic intuition, moral greatness and cessation of desires; there is also no attempt to show that the Upanishadic spirit is in any sense reason, or that it has in it any dialectic law through which it has evolved itself into the two illusory forms of subjective and objective categories. There is also no definite statement in the Upanishads that the world as such is illusion, or that it represents a necessary stage through which the spirit must express itself out of the necessity of some inner law of itself. The self in the Upanishads is no doubt self-complete, but this self-completion does not involve the notion of any process. This self-completion is merely its immediacy, its intuitive and unmediated character and its blissful nature. With Spinoza the infinite is the *causa sui*, that which is in itself and is conceived through itself, and matter and thought are regarded as being two of its attributes which are independent of each other. The individual minds are but derivatives from the infinite substance of God and are finite and so imperfect. But there is no idea of any process of change of the real, for everything that exists is deducible from the very nature of God and is, therefore, already contained in Him just as the properties of a triangle are contained in the nature of the triangle itself. Without going into further details of the complex philosophy of Spinoza, it may be pointed out that the Upanishadic idealism cannot be regarded as Spinozism, for the reality in the Upanishads is the inmost self of man; the world of matter and the world of thought cannot be regarded as being only its two independent attributes which are somehow deducible from its nature. Also, no external definition of the nature of reality is to be found in the Upanishads as a *causa sui*. The reality is no doubt a *causa sui* in the Upanishads, but that is not its fundamental characteristic. Its fundamental nature is regarded as being indescribable and unthinkable being, the pure perceiver, the pure bliss. On the whole the central doctrine of the Upanishadic philosophy seems to be an idealism of a mystical type, in which the innermost self is regarded as the highest reality, from which the world has somehow come into being or of which the world is a manifestation, and which is also somehow to be regarded as the inner controller of all natural forces. This inmost self is of the nature of the experience that we have in deep dreamless sleep, and it is that from which all experiences and all objective diversities have come into being and in which they would all lose themselves. It is this doctrine that the inmost self is the highest reality and that all else that we consider as real are but derivations from it, and that this reality can be grasped by self-control and spiritual intuition, which affirms the cardinal doctrine of the Upanishads. If one has to label it with any particular name, I should like to call it not subjective, objective, or absolute idealism, but mystical idealism. The way in which various problems arise out of this view has been suggested here and there, and I shall attempt to show how the interpreters of Upanishadic idealism tried to work out these problems and make consistent systems of philosophy out of it.

3. The earliest attempt at a consistent interpretation of the Upanishadic philosophy that is now available to us is the Brahmasūtra attributed to Bādarāyaṇa. But from references that are found in this work we see that various other writers, such as Kāśakritsna, Auḍulomi, Aśmarathya and others, had probably written treatises in which they attempted to explain the Upanishadic philosophy in their own ways. Not only are these treatises lost to us, but it is extremely difficult to understand exactly what Bādarāyaṇa's views were regarding the philosophy of the Upanishads. For this work contains a large number of sūtras which are strung together in the form of a book, and various commentators have tried to read their own views while interpreting these sūtras. Most of these sūtras are supposed to sum up certain discussions on the meaning of a number of

Upanishadic texts, and all interpretations are based on the assumption that all Upanishads preach one consistent system of thought. We have also no means at our disposal to verify or to ascertain how far the particular sūtras that are supposed to form a particular topic of discussion refer to particular Upanishadic passages referred to by commentators and not to other contents. But important schools of Buddhistic idealism had arisen before Bādarāyaṇa attempted his work, and as Bādarāyaṇa tried to refute some of these schools in establishing his own view of the Upanishadic philosophy it will be proper if the views of the interpreters of the Upanishadic idealism beginning from Bādarāyaṇa are taken up for consideration after the schools of Buddhistic idealism are first dealt with. An additional reason is to be found in the fact that the earliest commentator of the Brahma-sūtra that is now available to us is Śaṅkara, and he himself was so much under the influence of Buddhistic thought that he was called a crypto-Buddhist by many important writers who followed him. It seems therefore desirable that before we take up the interpretations of Upanishadic idealism I should first say something about the rise and growth of Buddhistic idealism; but even before that I think I ought to say something about the philosophy of the Geetā which, in my opinion, was very largely influenced by Upanishadic thought and which probably was written before the rise of Buddhist idealistic schools, as I have elsewhere tried to show.

4. The idealistic philosophy of the Geetā is based on an Upanishadic idea (Kaṭha I. 6. I), and the Geetā, revising it in its own way, says:

This is called the eternal Aśvattha tree with its roots high up and branches downwards, the leaves of which are the Vedas and he who knows this knows the Vedas. Its branches spread high and low, its leaves or sense-objects are nourished by the *guṇas*, its roots spread downwards tied with the knots of *karma*, the human world. In this world its true nature is not perceived, it is the beginning and it is the end, and the nature of its subsistence remains unknown; it is only by cutting this firmly rooted Aśvattha tree with the strong axe of unattachment that one has to seek that state from which when once achieved no one returns.

The Geetā explains this simile of God, but elaborates it by supposing that these branches have further leaves and other roots which take their sap from the grounds of human beings to which they are attached by the knots of karma. This means a duplication of the Aśvattha tree, the main and the subsidiary. The subsidiary one is an over-growth which has proceeded out of man and has to be cut asunder before one can reach the main tree. Read in the light of this idea, God is not only immanent but transcendent as well. The immanent part which forms a cosmic universe is no illusion or mirage but is an emanation, a development from God. The good and the evil, the moral and the immoral of this world are all from Him and in Him. The stuff of this world and its manifestations have their basis and essence in Him and are upheld by Him. The transcendent part, which may be said to be the root high up, which is the basis of all that has grown in this lower world, is thus the differenceless reality, the Brahman; but though the Brahman is again and again referred to as being the highest abode of the ultimate realisation, the absolute essence, yet God in His super-personality transcends even Brahman in the sense that Brahman, however great it may be, is only a constitutive essence in the complex personality of God. The all-perceiving nature of God and the fact that He is the essence and upholder of all things in this world are again and again emphasised in the Geetā in various ways. Thus Krishṇa says in the Geetā: "There is nothing greater than I. All things are held in me like pearls in the thread of a pearl garland; I am the liquidity in water, the light of the sun and the moon, the manhood in man, smell in earth, the heat of the sun, the intelligence in the intelligent, the heroism in the heroes, strength in the strong, and I am also the desires which do not transgress the path of virtue". Again, it is said: "In my manifested forms I am pervading the whole world; all beings exist completely in me but I do not exist in them. Yet so do I transcend them that none of the beings exist in me...I am the upholder of all beings. I do not exist in them and yet I am their procreator". In both these passages (Geetā, 9. 3–5) God's relation with man, by which He exists in us and yet does not exist in us and is not limited by us, is explained by the fact of the threefold nature of God; there is a part of Him which has been manifested as the inanimate nature and also as the animate world of living beings. It is with reference to this all-pervasive nature of God that it is said that as the air in the sky pervades the whole world so are all beings in Him. "At the end of each cycle (*kalpa*) all beings enter into my nature and again at the beginning of a cycle I create them. I create again and again through my nature." Three prakritis of God are referred to in the Geetā—the prakriti of God as cosmic matter, prakriti as the nature of God from which all life and spirit have emanated, and prakriti as māyā or the power of God from which the three guṇas have emanated. It is with reference to the operation of these prakritis that the cosmic world and the world of life and spirit may be said to be existing in God; but there is another form of God as the transcendent Brahman, and so far as this form of God is concerned, God transcends this sphere of the universe of matter and life. In another aspect of God, in His totality and super-personality, He remains non-existent as a creator and upholder of all, though it is out of a part of Him that the world has come into being. With reference to His transcendent part it is said: "The sun, the moon and the fire had been illuminated by me—it is my final abode from which, once achieved, no one returns". And again side by side with this it is said: "It is my part that forms the eternal soul in the living which attracts the five senses and the *manas* (mind) which lies buried in prakriti and which takes the body and comes out of it with the six senses just as the air takes fragrance out of flowers". And then God is said to be the controlling agent of all appearances in this world. Thus it is said: "By my energy I am upholding the world and all living beings; as fire in the bodies of living beings and aided by the *prāṇa* functions I digest the four kinds of food and the light in the sun, the moon and the fire". Again it is said: "I reside in the hearts of all; knowledge, forgetfulness and memory all come from me".

5. From these examples it is evident that the Geetā does not know that Pantheism, Deism and Theism cannot be jumbled up into one as a consistent philosophic creed, and it does not attempt to answer any objections that may be made against a combination of such opposite views. The Geetā not only asserts that all is God, but it also again and again repeats that God transcends all and is simultaneously transcendent and immanent in the world. The answer which seems to be implied in the Geetā against all objections to the apparently different views of the nature of God is that transcendentalism, immanentalism and pantheism lose their distinctive and opposite characters in the melting whole of the superpersonality of God. Sometimes in the same passage and sometimes in passages of the same context the Geetā takes in a pantheistic view, reverting in the same breath to a transcendental view or to a theistic view, and thus seeming to imply that no contradiction was felt in the different aspects of God as preserver and controller of the world, as the substance of the world, life and soul, and as the transcendent substratum underlying them all.

In order to emphasise the fact that all that exists, this world of existence, or all that has a superlative existence in good or bad, is God's manifestation, the Geetā is never tired of repeating that whatever is highest, best or even worst in things is God or God's manifestation. The Geetā does not attempt to reconcile the contradictory parts which constitute the complex super-personality of God. How are the unmanifested or *avyakta* part as Brahman, the *avyakta* part as the cosmic substratum of the universe, the prakriti part as the producer of the guṇas and the prakriti part as the *Jīvas* or individual selves to be combined and melted together to form a complex personality? If unmanifested nature is the ultimate abode of God, how can God, who as a person cannot be regarded as a manifestation of this impersonal reality, be considered to be transcendent? How can it be related with God as a person and with His diverse nature as the cosmic universe, Jīva and the Guṇas? The concepts of Brahman, Jīva, the unmanifested category from which the world proceeds and the Gūṇas are all found in the Upanishads in passages which are probably mostly unrelated, but the Geetā seems to take them all together and to consider them as constituents of *Īśvara* (God), which are also upheld by Him in his superior form in which He transcends and controls them all. In the Upanishads the doctrine of devotion can hardly be introduced, though here and there faint traces of it may be perceived. If the Upanishads ever spoke of Īśvara it is only to show His great majesty, power and glory as the controller and upholder of all. But the Geetā is steeped in the mystic consciousness of an intimate personal relation with God, not only as the majestic super-person, but as a friend and teacher with whom one could associate oneself for acquiring wisdom and the light of knowledge. God is the dearest of the dear and the nearest of the near, and His being can be felt so intimately that a man can live simply for the joy of his love for Him and in his deep love for Him; all his outward religious differences and works of life may shrink away as relatively unimportant. From this description of the philosophy of the Geetā it will be seen that it was based very largely on the teachings of the Upanishads, but instead of tackling the real philosophical problems it only combines the various elements of Upanishadic doctrines which seemingly come in conflict with one another and welds them all together in the conception of a superpersonal God. The thought is no doubt idealistic, but it is not the idealism of philosophy wrought with logical thought but the idealism of religion, effervescent with emotion.

6. The Geetā is supposed to belong to the *Ekāntī* school of the Vaishṇava Pāñcarātra, and in dealing with the philosophy of the Geetā I am reminded of an important school of thought which can be found in another Pāñcarātra work, called Ahirbudhnyasaṃhitā, which also seems to me to be pretty old and quite uninfluenced by the later philosophical speculations. According to Ahirbudhnyasaṃhitā God or Īśvara is conceived of as being, and next to Him is the category of the unchangeable, the Brahman, consisting of the sum-total of the purushas, the prakriti as the equilibrium of the guṇas and time (*kāla*). Time is regarded as the element that combines the prakriti with the purushas. It is said that the prakriti, the purushas and the time are the materials which are led to their respective works in producing the manifold universe by way of the development of the categories, through the will movement (*sudarśana*) of God. It is this one unchangeable purusha that appears as the many individual selves, and these selves are all the manifestations or parts of Lord *Vishṇu* or Īśvara. The will of Īśvara, otherwise called Sudarśana or *Saṃkalpa*, which is regarded as a vibratory thought-

movement, is the dynamic cause of the differentiation of prakriti into the various categories. Time is not identified here with this power, but is regarded as a separate entity, as an instrument through which the power acts. Yet this time has to be regarded as being of a transcendental nature and co-existent with purusha and prakriti, and is to be distinguished from time as moments or their aggregates, which latter is regarded as the *tamas* aspect of the category of *mahat*. The power of God is one; it is not a physical power, but a power that involves non-mechanical movement, which is in a sense homogeneous with God and is of the nature of pure self-determined thought (*svacchanda-cinmaya*); it is not, however, thought in the ordinary sense with particular contents and objects, but it is thought in potentiality, thought that has to realise itself in subject and object form, manifesting itself as a spiritual thought-movement (*jñāna-mūla-kriyātmā*); it is this spiritual movement that by self-diremption splits itself up (*dvidhā-bhāvaṃ*) as the thought of God (*saṃkalpa*), the determining (*bhāvaka*) and the passive objectivity (*bhāvya*) called the prakriti, and it is through the former that the latter developed and differentiated itself into the various categories mentioned above. What is meant by the vibratory movement of the thought of God is simply its unobstructive character, its character of passing entirely into actuality without any obstruction. It is the pure unobstructive flow of God's thought power that is regarded as His whole, idea or thought. The prakriti or world-substance is thus as much spiritual as God's thought; it only represents the part and activity and content of the thought of God, and it only has an opportunity of behaving as an independent category of materiality when by the self-diremption of God's power the thought-energy requires an objective through which it can realise itself. The power of God in its original state may be conceived to be pure stillness or pure vacuity, and it is out of this indestructible spontaneity that it begins to set itself in motion. And it is this spontaneity which springs out of itself and is described as the thought of God or its self-dirempting activity, its desire for being many. All creation proceeds out of this spontaneity; the creation is not differently described as an event which happened at a particular time, but it is eternal spontaneity and this power of God that reveals itself as eternal self-manifestation. Whatever is described as movement (*kriyā*), energy (*vīrya*), self-completeness (*tejas*), or strength (*bala*) of God are but the different aspects of this power. The strength of God consists in the fact that He is never tired or fatigued in spite of His eternal and continuous operation of creation; His energy (*vīrya*) consists in this, that though His power is split up as the material on which it acts, yet it does not suffer any change on account of that; His lustre of self-completeness (*tejas*) consists in this, that He does not wait for the help of any instrument of any kind for His creative operation; and it is the self-spontaneity of this power that is described as His agency (*kartṛitva*), as the creator of the world. God is described as being both of the nature of pure consciousness and of the nature of power. It is the all-pervasive consciousness of the mind that constitutes the omniscience of God, and when this wholeness, omniscience and self-complete consciousness as pure differenceless vacuity dirempts itself into the creative operation it is called His power. It is on this account that the power (*śakti*) of God is described as being thought-movement (*jñāna-mūla-kriyātmaka*). This power of consciousness may be regarded both as a part of God and therefore one with Him, and also as His specific character or quality. It is this power which dirempts itself as consciousness and its object (*cetya-cetanā*), as time and all that is measured by time (*kālya-*

kāla), as manifested and unmanifested (*vyaktāvyakta*), as the enjoyer and that which is enjoyed (*bhoktā-bhogya*), as the body and that which is embodied (*deha-dehī*). The conception of purusha seems to indicate the view of a creation or the formation of an association of individual selves like the honeycomb of the bees. They are regarded as unchangeable in themselves and yet they are covered over with the dusty impurities of beginningless instinctive root desires (*vāsanā*), and thus though pure in themselves they may also be regarded as impure. In themselves they are absolutely unaffected by any kind of afflictions, and being parts of God's nature are omniscient and eternally emancipated beings. These purushas, being of the nature of manifestations of the creative operation of God's power, are by His own will differently affected by ignorance (*avidyā*), which makes them subject to various kinds of afflictions; and as a result thereof their own natures are hidden from themselves. They thus appear to be undergoing all kinds of virtuous and sinful experiences of pleasures and pains; and being thus affected with these are first associated with the creative power of God. Then as the power first evolves itself into this first category of time as the all-determining factor (*niyati*), they become associated with that category, and then as the *sattva guṇas* gradually evolve from time, the *rajoguṇas* from sattva and the *tamoguṇas* from rajas, the purushas are associated first with sattva, then with rajas and then with tamas. When all the guṇas are evolved, though the three guṇas are then all disturbed for further creative operation, they are not disturbed in all the parts, and there are some parts of the guṇa-conglomeration which are in equilibrium with one another; this state of the equilibrium of the guṇas is called the prakriti. The honeycomb of the purushas thus forms a primal element which is associated with the self-evolving energy of God from the first moment of its movement, continues to be so associated with each of the evolving stages of categories up to the evolution of prakriti and later on with all the other categories that are evolved from prakriti. This conglomeration of the purushas is admitted to be the changeless substance that is associated with the evolution of the categories and descends gradually down through the successive stages of the categories until we come to the complete human stage of the evolution of the different senses of the gross elements. Unlike the kind of purusha that is found in the classical Sāṃkhya treatises, which regard the purushas as being absolutely untouched by the instinctive root desires (*vāsanā*) and the afflictions, it considers the purushas to be full of impurities of vāsanās and afflictions though in themselves they are essentially pure; again the classical Sāṃkhya considers that the vāsanās are produced in a beginningless way through karma through an endless series of births and rebirths, whereas in this system the different purushas are originally associated with different vāsanās according to the will of God. Unlike the kind of the classical Sāṃkhya where the vāsanās are regarded as part of prakriti as buddhi or *citta*, here they form an original extraneous impurity of the purushas.

7. A little consideration will show that this system of Vaishṇava thought may be regarded as an original interpretation of the Upanishadic Philosophy. It may be remembered that in the Upanishads we hear that the ultimate Brahman through a desire of becoming many performed tapas and through that created the universe. It may also be noted that in the Muṇḍaka Upanishad thought is described as being the tapas of Brahman (*jñānamayaṃ tapaḥ*), but this idea is only touched on there and not further developed in any of the earlier Upanishads. In some passages of the Upanishads it is said that Brahman perceived that he would be many and

thus he became many. In the Śvetāśvatara Upanishad it is said that thought-power or movement is spontaneous with God and, in the Taittirīya, Brahman is described as being the truth, the thought and the infinite. It seems clear that in the above system the power, will or perception of God is identified as spontaneous thought-movement; and it is in this way that the theistic view of a creation is reconciled with the pantheistic view of creation as spontaneous self-development of God. There is yet another element which has to be taken note of here. We remember that in the Atharvaveda (19. 54) time is regarded as a first god; it began the work of creation, and it is in time that both Brahman and tapas were upheld and time is regarded as the lord of all things. The whole universe was set in motion by time and produced by time, and it was time which became Brahman. This idea of the Atharvaveda was almost ignored in the Upanishads, and in the Śvetāśvatara the view that everything came out of time is regarded as a heretical doctrine. In the above system, however, time is identified with the thought-movement of God and is regarded as the first category of its inner movement, which is responsible not only for the creation of the cosmos but also of the colony of individual selves. We thus find here a system of dynamic absolutism in which the absolute out of the necessity of its own nature as thought spontaneously sets itself in movement, which is called its power, its will or time, and through it splits itself up into the subjective and the objective order. There is no particular point of time when this movement starts and there is no external cause which acts as its stimulant. The absolute is complete in itself and its movement is spontaneous; it is the spontaneity of this movement that is also regarded as its vision, and the necessity that is involved in its own nature otherwise called niyati is what determines the nature of the direction in which it flows; and it is also responsible for the specific natures of the subjective and the objective order that have sprung into being. The absolute, however, does not exist in its self-evolving activity, but remains in full self-possession even though it may be splitting itself up as consciousness of the unconscious series. The conscious series involving an infinite number of souls is associated throughout the whole course of evolution with the different grades of the objective category, until the fullest development of the latter is attained in the creation of the cosmos as we have it. The individual members of the colony of souls being parts of God are all absolutely pure and unchangeable, but yet through the divine practical necessity of the self-realisation through moral struggle in the cosmos they are all associated from the moment of their separation with God with extraneous limitations which formed a nucleus which would determine the nature of the future history in the form of root tendencies (vāsanās) from which it will be their duty to free themselves through their moral struggle in the world. In this system of thought the spirituality of matter and of individual souls is well established. The full reason of the association of matter and spirit is to be found in the fact that they are both jointly evolved out of the spontaneity of the absolute; they have both remained associated together at each of the stages of the development of the thought-movement of God as the spontaneous movement of the absolute. Throughout the whole course of the evolution they simply break up into two poles of the dialectic as the creator and the created, and the thinker and the thought. In a way it seems to me to be the best reconciliation of the apparently irreconcilable strands of Upanishadic thought, and it has indirectly inspired some of the most important Vaishṇava systems of thought that have been elaborated in later times. If I had to label it with any name I should call it "The idealism of dynamic pantheism".

8. But while the followers of the Upanishadic line of thought were thus trying to re-think the Upanishadic ideas and reconcile them in systematic forms in their own words, many other thinkers were trying to think out the problem of their time independently. Much of the history of these thinkers is now unknown to us, and it is to be seen how far our future researches can explore the nature of the intellectual activity of this period with any degree of exactness. Thus while the law of karma which started while the belief in the magical Vedic rites was being formulated in the Upanishadic period, and while the conviction was growing in the Upanishadic circles that the birth and experiences of a man were determined according to his deeds, we have evidences of schools of thought, known as the Ājīvakas, who continued to preach the nihilism of karma and who thought that there was no such thing as exertion or labour or power or energy or human strength and that all things were unalterably fixed. The Dighanikāya, while giving an account of the schools, says that according to them

> There is no cause either proximate or remote for the deprival of beings; they become deprived without reason or cause. There is no cause either proximate or remote for the purity of beings: they become pure without reason or cause. Nothing depends either on one's own efforts or on the efforts of others; in short, nothing depends on any human effort, for there is no such thing as power or energy or human exertion or human strength. Everything that thinks, everything that has senses, everything that is procreated, everything that lives, is destitute of force, power or energy. Their varying conditions at any time are due to fate, to their environment and their own nature. (Hoernle's translation.)

This is a sort of ethical nihilism that attempted to upset

the entire moral order which formed the firm bed-rock not only of the Upanishadic belief but also of other thinkers of the age. The existence of such lines of thought remarkably demonstrates the view that the period which succeeded the Upanishadic times was a period when bold adventures in independent thinking were being undertaken, and this is very definitely proved by the rise of the two great schools of philosophy, namely, those of Buddhism and Jainism.

9. Gautama Buddha was born in or about the year 560 B.C. in the Lumbini grove near the ancient town of Kapilavastu in the now dense terraces of Nepal. According to the legends it was foretold of him that he would enter upon the ascetic life when he should see "a decrepit old man, a diseased man, a dead man and a maniac". His father tried his best to keep him away from these by marrying him and surrounding him with luxuries. But on successive occasions while issuing from the palace he was confronted by these four things, which filled him with distress; and realising the impermanence of all earthly things he determined to forsake his home and try if he could discover some means of immortality to remove the sufferings of human beings. He made his "Great renunciation" when he was twenty-nine years old. He travelled on foot to Rājgriha and thence to Vārāṇasī where in company with other ascetics he entered upon a course of extreme self-discipline, carrying his austerities to such a length that his body became utterly emaciated and he fell down senseless and was believed to be dead. After six years of this great struggle he was convinced that the truth was not to be won by the way of extreme asceticism, and resuming an ordinary course of life he at last attained absolute and supreme enlightenment.

10. It is difficult to assert what exactly was the nature of his enlightenment. But what passed as the philosophy which the Buddha preached was the twelvefold chain of causation which is supposed to explain the mystery of the world. The early Buddhist philosophy did not accept any fixed entity or being as determining the nature of all realities. The only things that existed were the substantial phenomena, and these were called *dharmas.* But the question is, that if there is no substance or reality, how are we to account for the phenomena? But the phenomena are happening and passing away and the main point of interest with the Buddha was to find out; what being what else is, what happening what else happens, what not being what else is not. The phenomena are happening in a series, and we see that there being certain phenomena there become some others in relation to them or with reference to them. The question with which the Buddha started before attaining Buddhahood was this: In what miserable condition are the people; they are born, they decay, pass away and are born again, and they do not know the path of escape from this decay, death and misery. How to know the way of escape from this misery, decay and death? Then it occurred to him, what being there are decay and death, depending on what or with reference to what do they come? As he thought deeply it occurred to him that decay and death could only occur when there is birth, so they depend on birth. What being there is birth, on what does birth depend? Then it occurred to him that birth could only be if there were previous existence (*bhava*). But on what does then existence depend or what being there, there is bhava? Then it occurred to him that there could not be existence unless there is the "holding fast" (*upādāna*). But on what did upādāna depend? It occurred to him that it was desire (*taṇhā*). But what being there, can there be desire? To this question it occurred to him that there must be feeling (*vedanā*) in order that there may be desire. But on what does vedanā depend or rather what being there, there may be feeling (*vedanā*)? To this it occurred to him that there must be a sense-contact (*sparśa*) in order that there can be feeling. If there should be no sense-contact there would be no feeling. But on what does this sense-contact depend? It occurred to him that as there were six sense-contacts there were the six feelings of contact (*āyatana*). But on what did these six āyatanas depend? It occurred to him that there must be the mind and body (*nāmarūpa*) in order that there might be the six feelings of contact. But on what did the nāmarūpa depend? It occurred to him that without consciousness (*vijñāna*) there could be no nāmarūpa. But what being there, there would be vijñāna? Here it occurred to him that in order that there might be vijñāna there must be the affirmations (*saṇkhāra*) or synthesising activity of the complexes. But what being there, are there the saṇkhāras? Here it occurred to him that the saṇkhāras can only be if there is ignorance (*avijjā*). If avijjā can be stopped, then the saṇkhāras will be stopped, and if the saṇkhāras can be stopped, the viṇṇāna can be stopped, and so on. For our present purpose the question whether all these twelve links of causation were discovered by the Buddha himself in their entirety, or whether originally there was a lesser number of links to which some more were added in later times, need not detain us here, for whatever that may be it is certain that the spirit of the twelve links was present in the primitive formulation even though it may not have contained all the twelve links. But the most important protest against the Upanishadic thought that is to be found in the view that was enunciated by the Buddha consists in his radical denial of the existence of self. There was no ātman as a permanent entity, individual or being. What appears as self is only the aggregate of different elements such as the body and the senses, the feelings, conceptual knowledge, the synthetic functioning of combined sense-affections, combined feelings and combined concepts of the consciousness. Interpreting it according to later explanations, we find that the early Buddhistic thought was radically pluralistic; no permanence and no ultimate reality can be attributed to anything; but whether we take the subject or the object phenomena, we find that there is only a concourse of diverse elements which are momentarily coming together, disintegrating and forming new components, again disintegrating and forming other components, and so on. There is no distinction of substance and qualities, for what is called a substance is as much an element as that which is called a quality, and there is no reason why one entity should be dependent on another or should be considered as inherent in another; so the distinctions of substance and qualities and actions are ignored. The so-called substance, qualities and actions are placed on the same plane and taken as separate elements. Thus the elements cannot have any further description than the momentary form in which they appear, and there is no individual agent that persists through time, but each element, each component, lasts only for the moment in which it appears. The elements have this peculiarity that they act in co-operation with one another, and that such co-operation takes place in such a relative reference that there being some entities there are other entities. Since there is no permanent cause, no ground, no producer and no permanency anywhere, no conglomeration of entities can be called an individual or a cause. Cause is to be understood only in the sense of "This being there, that is". In the Upanishads we had the idea that an individual is composed of sixteen parts, of which the last part was a nucleus and the ground of all the rest. Here, however, there is no such ground part, and an individual is reduced to sense-data, cognitional feeling and consciousness-elements and the element of functioning by virtue of which the diverse elements would come together and show up the appearance of the individual. Since no ground can be affirmed of any of the elements that appear, all elements are absolutely unsubstantial, and there is no way of penetrating into them any further than their momentary appearance. It is only through avidyā that the conglomerations of these unsubstantial and impermanent elements are regarded as permanent or semi-permanent individuals.

11. The true self with the Upanishads was a matter of transcendental experience, for they said that it could not be described in terms of anything, but could only be pointed out as "there" behind all the changing mental categories. The Buddha looked into the mind and saw that it did not exist and the Buddha is represented as saying: "When one says 'I', what he does is that he refers either to all the elements combined or any one of them and deludes himself that that was 'I', just as one could not say that the fragrance of the lotus belongs to the colour so one could not say that the sense-data was 'I' or that the feeling was 'I' or that any of the other elements was 'I'. There is nowhere to be found in the elements composing an individual 'I am'". What people perceived in themselves when they said that they perceived their selves was but the mental experiences either individually or together. The Upanishads reveal through them the dawn of an experience of an immutable reality as the self of man, as the only abiding truth behind all changes, but Buddhism holds that this immutable self of man is a delusion and false knowledge. The first postulate of the system is that impermanence is sorrow. Ignorance about sorrow, ignorance about the way in which it originates, ignorance about the nature of the extinction of sorrow and ignorance about the

means of bringing about its extinction are the four kinds of ignorance (*avidyā*). The word avidyā also occurs in the Upanishads, but there it means ignorance about the ātman doctrine, and it is sometimes contrasted with vidyā or true knowledge about the self. With the Upanishads the highest truth was the permanent self, the bliss; but with the Buddha there was nothing permanent and all was change; and all change of impermanence was sorrow.

12. This early phase of Buddhism was thus a system of pluralistic phenomenalism, which did not attribute any greater importance to mind than to matter; and where mind and matter vanished as individual entities, we found in their place a number of elements (seventy-five according to the later elaboration of the system).

13. It may thus be difficult to conceive how from this doctrine there can originate any system of idealism, monism or absolutism, but a little inspection will show that this elimination of all substantiality and reality from the elements which are supposed to compose the so-called individual took away from them the basis of realism or realistic pluralism. The elements are no doubt as they are perceived, but we cannot say that they are real as they are perceived, for there is no reality behind them. When, therefore, the enquiring mind pursues the question, which naturally arises in the mind and without an answer to which the mind cannot be set at rest, "What is there behind these elements, what is the ground of these appearances, what is their substance?" and if such a question meets with the answer that there is no ground and no reality behind the elements, the elements are naturally reduced to mere appearances, and to the question, "What is the ultimate reality, what is truth?" the only answer that can be expected is that everything is void and essenceless; there is nothing real anywhere. The goal or *Nirvāṇa*, as held before us by early Buddhism according to the Theravāda interpretations, cannot show to us any positive element. The Buddha no doubt could not give any positive answer as to what becomes of us when the nirvāṇa is attained, for whether we exist in some form eternal, or do not exist, is not a proper Buddhistic question. For it is an heresy to think of a *Tathāgata* as existing eternally (*śāśvata*) or not existing, or whether he is existing as well as not existing, or whether he is neither existing nor non-existing. So anyone who seeks to discuss whether nirvāṇa is either a positive or eternal state, or a mere state of non-existence or annihilation, takes a view which has been discarded in Buddhism as heretical. We can only describe nirvāṇa according to the early Buddhism as extinction of sorrows, as the natural consequence of the destruction of desires. But in spite of all these the question may still remain irresistible—What is then the ultimate reality? We shall show in our next chapter with what acuteness the logical dialectic of Nāgārjuna tried to prove the unsubstantiality and essencelessness of all concepts and of all appearances, and in doing this he only supplemented the view that had been indefatigably emphasised and endlessly repeated in the Prajñāpāramitā works with a logical apparatus. We shall also see how this doctrine of the unsubstantiality of all elements and their reduction to mere phenomenal appearances made it easy for many thinkers, who probably had a Brahminic training or grounding in the Upanishads, to reduce these elements into mere mental ideas and to supplement them with a permanent nucleus as pure consciousness.

Chapter IV

BUDDHIST IDEALISM

1. I suggested in my last chapter that when the Theravāda school of Buddhism started the doctrine of the unsubstantiality and impermanence of all elements, one logical consequence of that would be that there was nothing real anywhere. So the highest truth would be a mere nothingness of all phenomena, but neither the Theravāda Buddhism nor its later product the Sarvāstivādins, which admitted the existence of all things, could give us a logical dialectic by which the essencelessness of all things could be proved. Both the Theravādins and the Sarvāstivādins, therefore, remained at a stage in which they only emphasised the existence of the impermanent elements, but did not push the doctrine of impermanence and unsubstantiality to its natural, logical consequence of nihilism. Thus none of the early thinkers tried to emphasise this part of the doctrine, and seceded from the Mahāyāna school as represented in the Prajñāpāramitā in which they preached the doctrine of nothingness of all phenomena as the greatest attainable truth. But it was only Nāgārjuna who first applied the Law of Contradiction to all phenomena and to all concepts and tried to establish the doctrine that no concepts could be explained either by themselves or by other entities; that all attempts to understand them would land us in confusion from which there is no escape, and that, therefore, all phenomena had only a relative appearance and at bottom were all essenceless, inconceivable and self-contradictory.

2. The Mādhyamika system of Nāgārjuna holds that there is nothing which has an essence or nature of its own; even heat cannot be said to be the essence of fire, for both the heat and the fire are the results of the combination of many conditions; what depends on many conditions cannot be said to be the single nature or essence of the thing. That alone may be said to be the true essence or nature of anything which does not depend on anything else, and since no such essence or nature can be discovered which stands independently by itself we cannot say that it exists. If a thing has no essence or existence of its own we cannot affirm the essence of other things of it. If we cannot affirm anything positive of anything we cannot consequently assert anything negative of anything. If anyone first believes in things positive and afterwards discovers that they are not so, he may be said to have faith in negation, but in reality since we cannot speak of anything as positive we cannot speak of anything as negative either. It may be objected that we nevertheless perceive things and processes going on. To this the Mādhyamika reply is that a process of change could not be affirmed of things that are permanent. But we can hardly speak of a process with reference to momentary things; for those which are momentary are destroyed the next moment after they appear, and so there is nothing which can continue to justify a process. That which appears as being neither comes from anywhere nor goes anywhere and that which appears as destroyed also does not come from anywhere nor goes anywhere, and so no process of change can be affirmed of beings either in their origination or in their destruction. It cannot be that when the second moment arose the first moment had suffered a change in the process, for it was not the same as the second and there was no so-called cause-effect relation. In fact, there being no relation between the two the temporal determination as prior and posterior is wrong. The supposition that there is a self which suffers changes is invalid, for there is neither self nor the so-called psychological elements. If the soul is a unity it cannot undergo any process, for that would suppose that the soul abandons one character and takes up another at the same identical moment, which is inconceivable. But then the question may arise that if there is no process and no cycle of worldly existence, what is then the nirvāṇa? Nirvāṇa, according to the Mādhyamika theory, is the absence of the essence of all phenomena which cannot be conceived either as anything which has ceased or as anything which is produced. In nirvāṇa all phenomena are lost; we say that the phenomena cease to exist in nirvāṇa, but like the illusory snake in the rope they never existed. Nirvāṇa is merely the cessation of the seeming phenomenal flow. It cannot, therefore, be designated either as positive or as negative, for these conceptions only belong to phenomena. In this state there is nothing which is known, and even the knowledge of the phenomena having ceased to appear is not found. Even the Buddha himself is a phenomenon, a mirage or a dream, and so are all his teachings.

3. The Mādhyamika school wishes to keep the phenomenal and the real views wide apart. If from the phenomenal view things are admitted to be as they are perceived, all the relations are also to be conceived as they are perceived. Thus while Diṅnāga urges that a thing is what it is in itself (*svalakshaṇa*), Candrakīrti, a follower of Nāgārjuna, holds that since relations are also perceived to be true, the real nature of things need not be svalakshaṇa; the relational aspects of things are as much true as the unrelational as well. Phenomenal substances exist as well as their qualities. "The thing-in-itself", says Nāgārjuna, "is as much a relative concept as all relational things that are popularly perceived to be true"; that being so, it is meaningless to define perception as being only the thing-in-itself. Candrakīrti thus

does not think that any good can be done by criticising the realistic logic of the Naiyāyikas. So far as the popular perceptions or conceptions go the Nyāya logic is quite competent to deal with them and to give an account of them. There is a phenomenal reality or order which is true for the man in the street and on which all our linguistic and other usages are based. It is, therefore, useless to define valid perception as being only the unique thing-in-itself and to discard all associations of quality or relations as being extraneous and invalid. Such a definition does not improve matters; for in reality such a definition is also relative and therefore false. Āryyadeva, another follower of Nāgārjuna, says that the Mādhyamika view has no thesis of its own which it seeks to establish, for it does not believe in the reality or unreality of anything or in the combination of reality or unreality. Thus there is no ultimate thesis in Nāgārjuna. It is, therefore, neither idealism nor realism nor absolutism, but blank phenomenalism which only accepts the phenomenal world as it is but which would not, for a moment, tolerate any kind of essence, ground or reality behind it.

4. As Buddhism was gradually developing, it began to make many converts from amongst the Brahmins who were trained in the Upanishadic learning. One of these was Aśvaghosha, the son of a Brahmin named Saiṃhaguhya, who spent his early days in travelling over the different parts of India and in defeating the Buddhists in open debates. He was probably converted into Buddhism by Pārśva, who was an important person in that age. He in all probability was a man steeped in the knowledge of the philosophy of the Upanishads, and after his own conversion into Buddhism he interpreted it in a new line which, together with the philosophy of the Laṅkāvatārasūtra, marks the foundation of Buddhist idealism. He held that in the soul two aspects

may be distinguished; the aspect as the reality (*bhūta-tathatā*) and the aspect as the cycle of birth and death. The soul as bhūtatathatā means the oneness of the totality of all things (*dharmadhātu*), i.e. that in which all the appearances ultimately merge and from which they have all come into the so-called being.[1] Its essential nature is uncreative and eternal. All things, simply on account of the beginningless traces of the incipient and unconscious memory of our past experiences of many previous lives, appear in their objective and individuated forms. If we could overcome this, our integrated history of past experiences, otherwise called vāsanā or smriti, the essence of all individuation and plurality, would disappear and there would be no trace of the world of objects. "Things in their fundamental nature are not nameable or explicable. They cannot be adequately expressed in any form of language. They possess absolute sameness (*samatā*). They are subject neither to transformation nor to destruction; they are nothing but one soul—thatness—reality (*bhūtatathatā*)." This "thatness" or reality has no attribute and it can only be somehow pointed out in silence as the mere "that". Since you understand that when the totality of existence is spoken of or thought of, there is neither that which speaks nor that which is spoken of, there is neither that which thinks nor that which is thought of, you have the stage of "thatness". This bhūtatathatā is neither that which is existent nor that which is non-existent, nor that which is at once existent and non-existent, nor that which is not at once existent and non-existent. It is neither that which is plurality, nor that which is at once unity and plurality, nor that which is

[1] The treatment of Aśvaghosha's philosophy is based upon Suzuki's translation of Aśvaghosha's Śraddhotpādasūtra. Whether Śraddhotpādasūtra can be attributed to Aśvaghosha or not need not be discussed here.

not at once unity and plurality. It is negative in the sense that it is beyond all that is conditional, and it is positive in the sense that it holds all within it. It cannot be comprehended by any kind of particularisation or distinction. It is only by transcending the range of our intellectual category and the comprehension of the limited range of finite phenomena that we can get a glimpse of it. It cannot be comprehended by the particularising consciousness of all beings, and we thus may call it negation (*śūnyatā*) in this sense. The truth is that which subjectively does not exist by itself, that the negation (śūnyatā) is also void (*śūnya*) in its nature, that neither that which is negation nor that which negates is an independent entity. It is the pure soul that manifests itself as eternal, permanent, immortal, which completely holds all things within it. On that account it cannot be called affirmation; and there is no trace of affirmation in it because it is neither the product of the creative function of thought nor the sub-conscious memory as the integrated past history of experiences, and the only way of grasping this truth—the thatness—is by transcending all conceptual creation. "The soul in birth and death comes forth from the tathāgata-womb, the ultimate reality. But the immortal and the mortal coincide with each other though they are not identical."

5. "Thus the absolute self remains a relative aspect by its self-affirmation. It is called the all-pervading mind (*ālayavijñāna*). It expresses two principles: (1) enlightenment, (2) non-enlightenment. Enlightenment is the perfection of the mind when it is free from the corruptions of the creative, instinctive, incipient memory. It penetrates all and is the unity." When it is said that all consciousness starts from this fundamental truth it should not be thought that consciousness had any real origin, for it was merely a phenomenal existence, a mere imaginary creation of the perceivers under the influence

of the delusive smṛti. The multitude of people are said to be lacking in enlightenment because ignorance (*avidyā*) prevails, because there is a constant influx of smṛti or past memory conserved as sub-conscious thought which forces itself constantly into the conscious plane and from which they are never emancipated; but when they are divested of this smṛti they can then recognise that no stages of mentation, viz. their appearance and presence, change and disappearance, have any reality. They are neither in a temporal nor in a spatial relation with the soul for they are not self-existent. This high enlightenment shows itself imperfectly in our grouped phenomenal experiences as *prajñā* (wisdom) and karma. By pure wisdom we understand that when one by virtue of the perfuming power of the dharma disciplines himself truthfully and accomplishes meritorious deeds, the mind (ālayavijñāna) which associates itself with birth and death would be broken down, and the modes of the evolving consciousness will be annulled and the power of the genuine wisdom of the dharmas will manifest itself.

Though all modes of consciousness and mentation are the mere products of ignorance, the ignorance in its ultimate nature is regarded as being both identical and non-identical with enlightenment; and, therefore, ignorance is in one sense destructible and in another sense indestructible. This may be illustrated by the simile of the water and the waves which are stirred up in the ocean. Here the water can be said to be both identical and non-identical with the waves. The waves have been stirred up by the wind but the water remains the same. When the winds cease the motion of the waves subsides but the water remains the same. Likewise, when the mind of all creatures which in its own nature is pure and clean is stirred up by the wind of ignorance (*avidyā*) the waves of mentality (*bhāvanā*) make their appearance. These three (the mind, ignorance and mentality), however, have no existence and they are neither unity nor plurality. When ignorance is annihilated the awakened mentality is tranquilised but the essence of wisdom remains unmolested.

The truth or the enlightenment is absolutely unobtainable by any modes of relativity or by any outward sense of enlightenment. All things in the phenomenal world are but reflections in the true light, so that they neither pass out of it nor enter into it and they neither disappear nor are destroyed. It is, however, disassociated from the mind (ālayavijñāna), which associates itself with birth and death, since it is in its true nature clean, pure, eternal, calm and immutable. This truth again is such that it transforms itself, wherever conditions are favourable, in the form of tathāgata or in some other forms, in order that all beings may be induced thereby to bring their virtue to maturity.

6. "Non-enlightenment has no existence of its own apart from its relation with enlightenment *a priori*." But enlightenment *a priori* is spoken of only in contrast with non-enlightenment, and as non-enlightenment is non-entity true enlightenment in turn loses its significance too. They are distinguished only in mutual relation as enlightenment or non-enlightenment. The manifestations of non-enlightenment are made in three ways: (1) as a disturbance of the mind (ālayavijñāna) by the action of ignorance producing misery, (2) by the appearance of an ego or a perceiver, and (3) by the creation of an external world which does not exist independently of the perceiver. Out of the unreal external world six kinds of phenomena arise in succession. The first phenomenon is intelligence; being affected by the external world the mind becomes conscious of the difference between the agreeable and the disagreeable. The second phenomenon is succession; following upon intelligence, memory retains the sensations agreeable as well as disagreeable in a continual succession of sub-

jective states. The third phenomenon is clinging; through the retention of a succession of sensations agreeable as well as disagreeable there arises the desire of clinging. The fourth phenomenon is an attachment to names or ideas, etc.; by clinging the mind hypostatises all names through which it gives definition to all things. The fifth phenomenon is the performance of deeds; on account of attachment to names, etc. there arise all the variations of deeds productive of individuality. The sixth phenomenon is the suffering due to the fetter of deeds; through deeds arises suffering in which the mind finds itself entangled and curtailed of its freedom. All these phenomena have thus come forth through avidyā or ignorance.

7. The relation between this truth and avidyā is in one sense a mere identity and may be illustrated by the simile of all kinds of pottery, which though different are all made of the same clay (compare Chāndogya Upanishad 6. 1. 4). Ignorance and its various transient forms all come from one and the same entity. Therefore, the Buddha teaches that all beings are from eternity abiding in nirvāṇa. It is by the touch of ignorance that the truth comes in the phenomenal form of existence.

8. In the all-surveying mind (ālayavijñāna) ignorance manifests itself, and from non-enlightenment starts that which sees, that which represents, that which apprehends an objective world and that which constantly particularises it into various individual forms. This is called ego (*manas*). Five different names are given to the ego according to its different modes of operation. The first name is activity-consciousness (*karmavijñāna*), in the sense that through the agency of ignorance an unenlightened mind begins to be disturbed. The second name is evolving-consciousness (*pravṛitti vijñāna*); it means that when the mind is disturbed there evolves that which sees an external world. The third name is representative-consciousness, which means that the ego (manas) represents or reflects an external world. As a clear mirror reflects the images of all descriptions, it is even so with the representative-consciousness; when it is confronted, for instance, with the objects of the five senses it represents them instantaneously and without effort. The fourth is particularising-consciousness, in the sense that it discriminates between different things, defiled as well as pure. The fifth name is succession-consciousness; it means that it is continuously attracted by the waking consciousness of attention. It (manas) represents all experiences and it never loses nor suffers through the destruction of any karma, good as well as evil, which had been done in the past and the retributions of which, painful or agreeable, are matured in the present or in the future; through this function the mind recollects things gone by and in imagination anticipates things to come. Since all things that are produced from ālayavijñāna are produced through the operation of the integrated history of experiences, all the modes of particularisation are the self-particularisations of the mind. The mind in itself, being however free from all attributes, is undifferentiated. Therefore, the conclusion is that all things and conditions in the phenomenal world get hypostatised and established only through ignorance of the integrated history of experiences and have no more reality than images in a mirror. They arise simply from the ideality of a particular mind. When the mind is disturbed, the multiplicity of things is produced, but when the mind is quiet, the multiplicity of things disappears. By ego-consciousness (*manovijñāna*) we mean the ignorant mind which by succession-consciousness clings to the conception of "I" and "not I" and misapprehends the nature of the objects of the six senses.

Thus, believing in the external world produced by the beginningless history of the integrated experiences, otherwise called vāsanā or smṛti, the mind becomes the principle of the sameness and undifferentiation that underlie all things which are one and perfectly calm and tranquil and show no sign of becoming.

9. Non-enlightenment is the *raison d'être* of saṃsāra, i.e. birth and rebirth. When this is annihilated the conditions of the external world are also annihilated, and with them the state of an unrelated mind is also annihilated. But this annihilation does not mean the annihilation of the mind but of its modes only. It becomes calm, like an unruffled sea when all winds which were disturbing it and producing the waves have been annihilated. In describing the relation of the interaction of avidyā (ignorance, karmavijñāna, activity-consciousness—the subjective mind), vishaya (external world represented by the senses) and the tathatā (thatness of the reality), Aśvaghosha says that there is an interpenetration or interperfuming of these elements. Thus Aśvaghosha says:

By perfuming we mean that while our worldly clothes have no odours of their own, neither agreeable nor disagreeable, they could yet acquire one or the other odour according to the nature of the substance with which they are perfumed. This thatness (tathatā) is likewise a pure dharma free from all defilements of the perfuming power of the ignorance. On the other hand, ignorance has nothing to do with purity. Nevertheless, we speak of being able to do the work of purity because it in its turn is perfumed by the "thatness". Determined by the "thatness" ignorance becomes the *raison d'être* of all forms of defilement, and then ignorance perfumes the "thatness" and produces the integrated history of experiences. This last again in its turn perfumes ignorance. On account of this reciprocal perfuming the truth is misunderstood; on account of its being misunderstood an external world of subjectivity appears. Further, on account of the perfuming power of memory various modes of individuation are produced, and by clinging to them various deeds are done, and as the result thereof we suffer miseries, mental as well as bodily. Again, the "thatness" perfumes ignorance and in consequence of this perfuming the individual in subjectivity is made to loathe the misery of birth and death and to seek after the blessing of nirvāṇa. This longing and loathing on the part of subjective mind in turn perfumes the "thatness". On account of this perfuming influence we are unable to believe that we are in possession within ourselves of the "thatness" whose essential nature is pure, and we also recognise that all phenomena in the world are nothing but the illusory manifestations of the mind (ālayavijñāna) and have no reality of their own. Since we thus rightly understand the truth, we can practise the means of liberations and can perform those actions which are in accordance with the dharma; we should neither particularise nor cling to objects of desire. By virtue of this discipline and habit we get ignorance annihilated after a lapse of innumerable years. As ignorance is thus annihilated the mind (ālayavijñāna) is no longer disturbed so as to be subject to individuation; as the mind is no longer disturbed the particularisation of the surrounding world is annihilated. When in this way the truth of the condition of defilements, their products and the mental disturbances are all annihilated, it is said that a person attains nirvāṇa.

10. The nirvāṇa philosophy is not nothingness, but *tathatā* or thatness in its purity, unassociated with any kind of disturbance which produces all the diversities of experience. The main idea of this tathatā philosophy seems to be that this transcendent thatness is at once a quintessence of all thought and activity; as avidyā veils it or perfumes it the world-appearance springs forth, but as the pure thatness also perfumes avidyā there is a striving for the good as well. As the stage of avidyā is passed this illuminating character shines forth, for it is the ultimate truth in which the illusion appears as the many of the world.

11. We see here that after the analogy of the Brahman in the Upanishads Aśvaghosha admitted one permanent reality from which he sought to derive everything else. We remember there are many passages in the Upanishad where the Brahman is described as being unthinkable, unspeakable and unnameable, as one that can only be indicated by negating all affirmations about it. The Māṇḍukya Upanishad, in trying to discover it, says that it is invisible, indefinable, unthinkable, which can have no practical bearing, wherein all appearances have ceased, one that is to be regarded as the soul. The dialectic of Nāgārjuna has made us familiar with the view that no affirmation of any kind, be it that of existence or of non-existence or of both, can be made of any entity, and that all appearances are impermanent and unsubstantial. Aśvaghosha seems to combine these two ideas into the doctrine that there is a reality which he calls the mere thatness, of which it is not possible to make any kind of affirmation or negation; and following the footsteps of the Upanishads he describes it as forming the essential nature of the soul. The question may arise, if any affirmation or negation of any kind be possible, how can this ultimate principle be regarded either as ultimate or as reality? Aśvaghosha seems to evade this charge by describing it as a mere thatness, and he thinks that by so doing he forbears from making any positive or negative affirmation regarding it. But he forgets that as a Buddhist he exposes himself to the charge of heresy by admitting a permanent entity as the ultimate truth. We have seen that in the Upanishads the word avidyā is used merely in the sense of ignorance of the superior philosophy. But the Buddha uses the term as the primary notion in the twelvefold link of causation. But here also avidyā is only a term in a revolving series, such that when there is the avidyā there are the saṃkhāras which represent the past deeds; and

there being avidyā and saṃkhāras in the past life, there are the *vijñāna*, *nāmarūpa*, *sparśa*, *vedanā*, *tṛshṇā*, *upādāna* and *bhava* in the present life, and then again the *jāti* and *jarāmaraṇa* in the next life.[1] The causality of avidyā towards the *saṃkhāra* does not imply any generative character or productive agency, for such notions are ruled out from the Buddhist notion of causality as defined by *pratītyasamutpāda*. When one says that there being avidyā there is the saṃkhāra, what is meant is that saṃkhāra arises associated with avidyā in the sense that when avidyā arises it is followed by the saṃkhāra. But this does not mean that avidyā is the material cause or a productive agent of saṃkhāras. It means only ignorance in the sense of passions or afflictions contrary to right knowledge. Avidyā is not a mere negation of knowledge or ignorance, but it is a positive entity in the sense of false knowledge. Yet it is not a substance which generates the saṃkhāras by itself or through itself, but it is its cause only in the sense that there being the avidyā there are the saṃkhāras. The concept of avidyā in Aśvaghosha is different from this notion of avidyā as we find in early Buddhism and its later interpretations by the Sarvāstivādins. Avidyā with Aśvaghosha appears as a dynamic agent, through the influence of which the ultimate reality, the "thatness", takes a creative attitude, at which stage it is called ālayavijñāna; yet this dynamic agent is not different in its ultimate character from the nature of "thatness", and the nature of "thatness" is itself indefinable by any affirmation or negation of any kind. The older concept, in which avidyā stood as only a term in a revolving series, is thus changed in Aśvaghosha's philosophy into a principle of activity. But it retains somehow its primitive character; because it is only through it that the past history of an individual in the form of root-potencies of

[1] See *A History of Indian Philosophy*, by S. N. Dasgupta, p. 84 et seq.

unconscious memory is retained; and it is through this that the "thatness" is made dynamic into the state of ālayavijñāna. It is through this ālayavijñāna that the appearance of the egos or perceivers and a false creation of an external world (the entire existence of which depends on the perception of these perceivers) are possible. It is in relation to this ālayavijñāna that the six kinds of phenomena, viz. of sensation, agreeable or disagreeable affections, desires, association of names and ideas, deeds and suffering, arise. Since without avidyā there would not have been the first stir into activity of the ultimate "thatness" into ālayavijñāna, and its successive developments as the egos and the ego-creations of the external world would have been impossible, the avidyā may still be regarded here as a first term of the revolving series, though here its dynamic character is more emphasised. It is through the influence of this avidyā that there starts that which sees, that which represents, that which apprehends an objective world and that which constantly particularises—the ego or manas. It is through the influence of this avidyā that the ego operates in its fivefold functions by which it rouses itself as ego, as the perceiver of an external world, as a thinker of ideas generated by the external world, as discriminating between good and bad and as retaining within itself all experiences that it gathers, whose good and bad effects it reaps. Avidyā thus produces this ego-appearance and through this ego-appearance generates the history of experiences of this ego-appearance, and through that there is the cycle of new ego-appearances, their new experiences and their newer and newer conserved history of experiences. The existence of the external world is but a perception of the ego, and the ego is the product of the history of the experience and its historically prior egos. Though the avidyā, the subjective minds and the external world which is but their perception, are all appearances or modes which in their ultimate nature are identical with the "thatness", yet by an intermixture or inter-penetration of them all we have an explanation of the individual person and his experiences. Thus, since the external world, its representation in the form of mental ideas, and the conservation of experiences are all due to the diverse kinds of ego operation, the system of Aśvaghosha may be regarded as subjective idealism with reference to the ego. But since the ultimate reality is only the indefinable "thatness", which is a reality even above the absolute mind of which the ego may be regarded as a manifestation, the system may be regarded as pure absolutism. And yet from the point of view that from one ālayavijñāna or absolute mind all the egos have been manifested, and that through the egos the world has been manifested, the system may be regarded also as absolute idealism.

12. I may now turn to the idealism of the Laṅkāvatāra-sūtra. According to this work, the author of which is unknown to us, all the dharmas or phenomenal entities are but imaginary constructions of the human mind. There is no motion in the so-called external world as we suppose, for no such world exists. We construct it ourselves, and then we ourselves are deluded that it exists by itself. There are two functions involved in our consciousness, that which holds the perceptions, and that which orders them by imaginary construction. The two functions, however, mutually determine each other and cannot be separately distinguished. These functions are set to work on account of the beginningless instinctive tendencies inherent in them in relation to the world of appearances. All sense-knowledge can be stopped when the diverse unmanifested instincts of imagination are stopped. All our phenomenal knowledge is without any essence or truth and is but a creation of māyā, a mirage or a dream. There is nothing

which may be called external, but all are the imaginary creations of one's own mind which has been accustomed to create imaginary appearances from beginningless time. This mind by whose movement these creations take place as subject and object has no appearance in itself and is thus without any origination, existence and extinction, and is called the ālayavijñāna. What is meant by this ālayavijñāna, which is said to be without origination, existence and extinction, is probably this, that it is always a hypothetical state which merely explains the phenomenal states that appear, and therefore has no existence in the sense in which the term is used and we cannot form any special notion of it.

13. We do not realise that all visible phenomena are of nothing external but of our own minds, and there is also the beginningless tendency for believing and creating a phenomenal world of appearances. There is also the nature of knowledge (which takes things as the perceiver and the perceived), and there is also the instinct in the mind which experiences diverse forms. On account of these four reasons there are produced in the ālayavijñāna the ripples of our sense-experience as in a lake, and these are manifested in sense-experiences and the five *skandhas* called *pañchavijñānakāya* in a proper synthetic form. None of the phenomenal knowledge that appears is either identical with or different from the ālayavijñāna, just as the waves cannot be said to be either identical with or different from the ocean. As the ocean dances on in waves so the citta or the ālayavijñāna is also dancing as it were in its diverse operations. As citta it collects all movements within it, as manas it synthesises and as vijñāna it constructs the fivefold perceptions. It is only due to māyā or illusion that the phenomena appear in their twofold aspect as subject and object. This must, however, always be regarded as an appearance, and one can never say whether they really existed or not. All phenomena, both being and non-being, are illusory. When we look deeply into them we find that there is an absolute negation of all appearances, including even all negations, for they are also appearances. This would make the ultimate truth positive; but this is not so, for it is that in which the positive and the negative are one and the same. Such a state, which is complete in itself and has no name and no substance, is described in the Laṅkāvatārasūtra as "thatness". This state is also described in another place in the Laṅkāvatārasūtra as voidness, which is one and has no origination and no essence. It may be supposed that this doctrine of an unqualified ultimate truth comes near to the vedantic ātman, and we find in the Laṅkāvatārasūtra that Rāvaṇa asks Buddha: "How can you say that your doctrine of *Tathāgatagarbha* is not the same as the ātman doctrine of the other schools of philosophy, for these heretics all consider the ātman as the eternal agent, unqualified, all-pervading and unchanged?" To this Buddha is supposed to reply thus:

> Our doctrine is not the same as the doctrine of those heretics. It is in consideration of the fact that the instructions of a philosophy, which considered that there was no soul or substance in anything, will frighten the disciples that I say that all things are in reality the tathāgatagarbha. This should not be regarded as ātman. Just as clay is made into various shapes so are the non-essential nature of all phenomena and their freedom from all characteristics, and this is described as the garbha or the *nairātmya* (essencelessness). This explanation of the tathāgatagarbha as the ultimate truth and reality is given in order to attract to our creed those heretics who are superstitiously inclined to believe in the ātman doctrine.

14. Thus Buddha explained the doctrine of *pratītyasamutpāda* with certain modifications. There was an external pratītyasamutpāda just as it appeared in the objective aspect and an internal pratītyasamutpāda. The external pratītyasamutpāda is represented in the way in which material things came into being by the co-operation of diverse elements—the lump of clay, the potter, the wheel, etc. The internal pratītyasamutpāda was represented by *avidyā*, *tṛshṇā*, *karma*, the *skandhas* and the *āyatanas*.

Our understanding is composed of two categories called the *pravicayabuddhi* and the *vikalpalakshaṇagrahābhiniveśapratishṭhāpikābuddhi*. The *pravicayabuddhi* is that which always seeks to take things in either of the following four ways: that they are either this or the other; either both or not both; either are or are not; either eternal or non-eternal. But in reality none of these can be affirmed of the phenomena. The second category consists of that habit of the mind by virtue of which it constructs diversities and arranges them (created in their turn by this constructive activity—*parikalpa*) in a logical order of diverse relations of subject and predicate, cause and other relations. He who knows the nature of these two categories of the mind knows that there is no external world of matter, and that they are all experiences in the mind only. There is no water, but it is the sense-construction of the perceivers that constructs the water as an external substance; it is the sense-construction of activity or energy that constructs the external substance of fire; it is the sense-construction of movement that constructs the external substance of air. In this way, through the false habit of taking the unreal as real, five skandhas appear. If these were to appear all together we could not speak of any kind of cause or relation, and if they appear in succession there can be no connection between them as there is nothing to combine them together. In reality there is nothing which is produced or destroyed. It is only our constructive imagination that builds up things as perceived by us, and ourselves as perceivers. Whatever we designate by speech is mere speech-construction and therefore unreal. In speech one could not speak of anything without relating things in some kinds of cause or relation, but none of these characters may be said to be true; the real truth can never be referred to by such speech-construction.

15. The nothingness (śūnyatā) of things may be viewed in seven aspects: (1) That they are always interdependent and hence have no special characteristics by themselves, and as they cannot be determined in themselves they cannot be determined in terms of others; for their own natures being only an undetermined reference to an "other" are also undetermined in themselves, and hence they are all indefinable. (2) That they have no positive essence, since they spring up from a natural non-existence. (3) That they are of an unknown type of non-existence, since all the skandhas or psychological groups vanish in the nirvāṇa. (4) That they appear phenomenally as connected though non-existent, for the skandhas have no reality in themselves nor are they related to others, and yet they appear to be somehow causally connected. (5) That none of the things can be described as having any definite nature; they are all undemonstrable by language. (6) That there cannot be any knowledge about them except that which is brought about by the longstanding defects of desires which pollute all our vision. (7) That things are also non-existent, in the sense that we affirm them to be in a particular place and time in which they are not. There is thus only non-existence, which again is neither eternal nor destructible and the world is but a dream and mirage; the two kinds of negation are ākāśa and nirvāṇa; things which are neither existent nor non-existent are only imagined to be existent by fools. This view apparently comes into conflict with the doctrine of this school that the reality is called tathāgatagarbha (the

womb of all that is merged in "thatness"), and all the phenomenal appearances and the psychological groups (*skandhas*), elements (*dhātus*) and fields of sense-operations (*āyatana*) only serve to veil it with impurities and this would bring it nearer to the assumption of a universal soul as reality, but the Laṅkāvatāra attempts to explain away this conflict by suggesting that the reference to the tathāgatagarbha as the reality is only a sort of false bait to attract those who are afraid of listening to the nairātmya doctrine.

16. As a matter of fact the Laṅkāvatāra seems to criticise the tathatā doctrine of Aśvaghosha (p. 108), where it says that others describe the uncreated, indestructible voidness of the eternal reality as "thatness". It is necessary, therefore, to compare and contrast the idealism of Aśvaghosha with that of the Laṅkāvatāra-sūtra. The tathatā or "thatness" of Aśvaghosha is sometimes described as nothingness or śūnyatā only because there is no distinction of reality of any kind in it; and because it is completely free from any attributes which are ascribed to ordinary things which are to be regarded as unreal, but at the same time it contains in itself infinite merit because it is self-existent, whereas the ultimate reality being in itself oneness, the totality of all things, and the great all-including whole, it is free from all projections of our subjective self, which invents relation and thereby makes all things appear as mutually related and individuated. The things in their ultimate nature possess no signs of distinction, and as such there is no transformation, destruction or distinction of any kind; all things in their essence are but the one soul for which the name tathatā or "thatness" is a convenient symbol. All words and expressions are nothing but representations projected forward by our subjective self and are not therefore realities. It is in this sense that the ultimate reality is to be regarded as unspeakable.

When this ultimate reality is described as negation, what is meant is that it is free from all signs of distinction existing among phenomenal objects. So in one sense this ultimate reality may be called that which is neither existent (in the popular sense in which all the diverse phenomenal appearances appear as existent) nor that which is non-existent (because it is the ground, the being and the essence of all things and in its own nature as such all things are identical with it as this alone forms their reality). It is not also that which is at once existent and non-existent (because none of the diversities of the manifold world exist in it). It is not also that which is not at once existent and non-existent (because in its existent form as ultimate reality it comprehends the essence of all being). It cannot be called mere unity because all duality and multiplicity have their ultimate being in it, and it cannot be called plurality because all notions of plurality are but false creations. It is on this account that there is no word in our phenomenal use by which we can describe the nature of this ultimate substance, for all words are relational and, being relational, they are the production of our particularising consciousness which is the source of all illusion.

17. In refuting the false interpretations of the mahāyāna doctrine Aśvaghosha says that hearing from the Mahāyāna-sūtra that the tathāgatagarbha is described as perfectly tranquil, there are ignorant people who think that the nature of the tathāgatagarbha is eternal and omnipresent in the same sense as space is regarded as eternal and omnipresent. But this cannot be, for, where there is the perception of space there is side by side a perception of a variety of things in contradistinction to which space is spoken of as if existing independently, for space exists only in relation to our particularising consciousness. Again, he points out that hearing from the Mahāyāna-sūtras that all things in the world are perfect emptiness (*atyanta śūnyatā*), that even nirvāṇa or suchness is also perfect emptiness and is devoid in its true nature of all characteristics, ignorant people cling to the view that nirvāṇa is a nothing and devoid of all contents. But this cannot be, for the ultimate reality is not a nothing, but holds within itself all infinite qualities which make up its true nature. He again points out that hearing from the sūtras that the tathāgatagarbha holds within it all qualities which do not suffer any increase or diminution in it, it is held by ignorant people that in the tathāgatagarbha there is an inherent and fundamental distinction such as is found between object and subject or matter and mind. But this cannot be, for the ultimate reality is devoid of all distinctions. Then again, he points out that hearing from the sūtras that even all impure and defiled things in the world are produced from the tathāgatagarbha, and that the things of the world are not different from it, it is held by ignorant people that this ultimate reality contains within it all objects of the world in their varied and pluralistic nature. But this cannot be, for the so-called pluralities of the world have no self-existence and are simply illusory, and therefore in a way the ultimate reality is wholly untouched by them. He, therefore, points out that there are many Buddhists who think that the Buddha taught the doctrine of a non-personal ātman as separate from the psychological clusters or skandhas which are momentary, but the true point of view is that all these psychological clusters are neither created nor annihilated. They are in their ultimate reality the essence, the nirvāṇa, and there is no impersonal ātman outside them which has to be achieved by our efforts. As soon as we free ourselves from our particularising tendencies we find that matter, mind, intelligence, consciousness, being and non-being, are all but relative terms, which in their apparent nature are inexplicable and which in their inner essence are identical with the ultimate reality, the "thatness". The "thatness" alone, therefore, is the ultimate reality (*tattva*), and this reality is absolutely beyond the realm of relations. All so-called illusory phenomena are in truth from the beginning what they were, and their essence is nothing but the one soul, the ultimate reality; and though ordinary people may regard this world of plurality to be true and real, wise persons always consider it to have an appearance only originating from the particularising consciousness of our minds, whereas in their ultimate essence they have but one reality, the "thatness". We now see that the doctrine of Aśvaghosha admits one reality as ultimate, absolute and true; all the rest are mere phenomena, which though false in all their appearances as many are yet identical in their ultimate essence with this absolute, which for want of specification is signified by the term "thatness".

18. The difference of this view from that of the Laṅkāvatāra may now become evident. The Laṅkāvatāra does not seem to admit any ultimate reality which may be regarded as absolute-in-itself. It thinks that all the diverse phenomena are simply appearances to each individual mind. The individual mind itself in its turn is also not an ultimate reality, but is itself an appearance. The appearances are neither caused nor destroyed, for the very notion of cause and production is false and is a mere appearance. According to the Laṅkāvatāra the whole of the wrong philosophy that has found currency amongst the people depends on the projection or assumption of false categories such as being, non-being, cause, effect, production, destruction, interaction, correlation, and the like. All these are mere false appearances to one's own mind; and we know that the mind is also in itself nothing but a false appearance. When the Laṅkāvatāra, therefore, describes all phenomena to be false, it is not to be supposed that it presumes the existence of any reality of any kind as distinct from the falsehood. The word falsehood has only value in contrast with the notion of reality, and as both these notions have the same status, being nothing but appearance, there is no ultimate meaning also in calling all phenomena false. All that can be said of the phenomena is that there is nothing behind them and that all doctrines of causation and all existence are meaningless and inexplicable. All things are neither existent nor non-existent (*sadasat-pakshavigata*), neither created nor destructible, neither positive nor negative. There is no movement anywhere. No one hears anything nor is anything heard, no one sees anything nor is anything seen. Just as an image in the mirror can neither be said to have been originated nor destroyed, neither existent nor non-existent, but is mere illusory perception, so is this entire world. Thus in one passage (p. 176) it is said that a Brahmin spoke to the Buddha that everything was produced, and the Buddha replied that this was a popular view. The Brahmin then said that nothing is produced, and the Buddha replied that this is the second popular view. Then when the Brahmin said that everything is non-eternal or everything is eternal or everything can be produced or nothing can be produced, the Buddha replied that these are all popular views. The Buddha further said that the notion of oneness, otherness, togetherness and the notion of neither the one nor the other, the notion that everything depends on causes, that everything is a modification, that there is something which is not a modification, that there is a self or that there is not a self, that there is this world or there is not the other world, that there is emancipation or that there is no emancipation, that everything is momentary or that nothing is momentary, all these views are mere popular views. The Buddha said that he did not believe in the doctrine of causes nor in the doctrine that there are no causes. He could not grasp these views because they are obsessed with the notion of reality, the notion of a self and its object and the notion of diverse relations. According to the Laṅkāvatāra, therefore, there is nothing real anywhere; everything, including all logical categories and relations of all kinds, is merely a perceptual appearance. Since all percepts, relations and all kinds of phenomena are but mere perceptual appearances, no affirmation of any kind can be made in any sphere. Metaphysical discussions are possible because the notions of unity, plurality, cause, effect, correlation and the like are regarded in a sense more primary than the data to which they are applied; but if all relations and all phenomena are mere perceptual appearances, none of which has a superior value to the others, it is impossible that any metaphysical speculation can be made regarding the nature either of such relations or of the phenomena to which they are to be applied. There cannot also be any notion of anything in itself, for the very notion of a thing-in-itself is a mere perceptual appearance and, as such, is not more primary than other appearances. Thus on p. 108 the question is asked of the Buddha whether illusion has any existence or not, and the Buddha replies that it is impossible to say whether illusion exists or not, for if the category of existence and non-existence can be applied to any entity, then that implies that the category of existence or non-existence is more primary than the illusion, and that indicates an obsession of the mind which in the proper perspective ought to be got rid of. Otherwise the Buddhist doctrine would be similar to the doctrine of other philosophers who believe in the application of these categories. For it is said that illusion is like the principle of māyā, which may explain the origin of other notions. Then this philosophy would believe in the productivity of māyā and would thus be similar to other systems of philosophy. All appearances are but delusion of the mind due to some wrong tendencies. The seers never perceive any illusion nor any reality beyond it, for if there is any reality beyond illusion, then illusion itself would be a reality, being the other side of the reality. If the ultimate cause is beyond the illusory, then that illusion may be regarded as the cause of that reality, just as darkness may be regarded as a cause of light. There is no category which can be called māyā, because all entities or appearances being similar to magic they are called māyā. All things are called similar to māyā because they are false and as evanescent as lightning sparks. All philosophers who believe in the existence of the entities speak of them as being produced out of something, but as Buddhism does not believe either in entities or in cause or in production, it cannot say of any entity or appearance that it has been produced or that it has not been produced, the whole notion of production and non-production being entirely alien to its doctrines. This view, however, seems to come into conflict with the view described before, and the Laṅkāvatāra philosophy admits the subjective mind, called the ālayavijñāna, from which through beginningless roots of desire there arise the creation of sense-data and their relations, and so also the external world as well as the inner experiences. There this ālayavijñāna is described as if it was the sea in which ripples arose, and these ripples were the subjective creations, the sensations and their relations. This would seem to indicate that the Laṅkāvatāra believed in the existence of a subjective mind; and if this was so, the philosophy just described, that nothing can be associated with any kind of reality and that everything was but meaningless phenomena about which no affirmations of any kind can be made, would be unobtainable.

19. The reconciliation of both the views, however, can be found in the fact that two kinds of philosophy are preached in the Laṅkāvatāra, a lower and a higher. As the higher philosophy is too radical, it was felt that it might scare away the ordinary people who were obsessed with the notion of some kind of reality, and it is for getting their minds prepared that the theory of a subjective mind from which everything else has come into being as modifications of it or as phenomena arising out of it, like a sea manifesting itself in waves and ripples, has been taught. The right view of the Laṅkāvatāra, however, is the higher philosophy, which would regard all logical and ontological notions to be but mere appearances, and would thus refute in the strongest terms any affirmation of reality regarding a subjective mind. Those who are familiar with European philosophy know well that according to Kant all logical notions are regarded as having emanated from the categories of the mind, and as such they could only be affirmed within experience but not beyond it. Kant, however, rather inconsistently admitted an unknowable extra-experiential source of our sensations. The Laṅkāvatāra carries Kant's programme to its logical extreme and regards all logical relations and all ontological, perceptual and psychological entities as possessing the same kind of status and validity in experience. As such it was impossible to make any metaphysical assertion of any kind regarding these entities. All entities are simply as they are; no further ultimate characterisation of their nature is possible, for all characterisation would be but mere appearance; still from the ordinary experiential view it can be imagined that all our experiences, including sensations and relations, have originated from a subjective mind. But since no affirmation can be made regarding any of the entities in our experience, which would be valid in itself or both in and beyond the experience and the experiential facts, they would be meaningless, inexplicable and unpredicable phenomena only. It is in this way, then, that the apparently conflicting views of the Laṅkāvatāra may be reconciled according to its own statement.

20. According to Aśvaghosha's philosophy we have both an ultimate reality as tathatā and a phenomenal mind which is subjective in its nature depending upon it. Though the reality of the phenomenal mind may be denied in its own nature as mere subjective mind with its root-tendencies and their creative developments as subjective mental phenomena, and their objective counterparts as the external world, yet the subjective mind is still real in its essence as ultimate "thatness". Both the philosophy of the Laṅkāvatāra and that of Aśvaghosha seem to be familiar with the Upanishadic theory of causation (such as the production of diverse kinds of earthen pots from a lump of earth), and this view seems to have been very well utilised in the philosophy of Aśvaghosha. But it is the special feature of Aśvaghosha's philosophy that though he regards all modifications of the original cause either as subjective mind in the first grade or its second grade developments as the external world and the mental phenomena as false, yet he thinks that the original cause has in itself all the diverse qualities by virtue of which such productions were possible. And this does not take away its undifferentiated character as mere distinctionless self-identity. No proper discussion is found regarding the question whether the ālayavijñāna can be regarded as one or many. Perhaps he does not consider it to be very important, but it seems that the ālayavijñāna, though often used in the singular, is used generically to denote the individual subjective centres of self which are associated with their own peculiar beginningless history of experiences and root-tendencies. The philosophy of the

Laṅkāvatāra has to be distinguished from that of Aśvaghosha in this, that the former may be regarded as being under the very influence of Nāgārjuna; and as a matter of fact the Laṅkāvatāra refers to Nāgārjuna as having formulated its philosophy (p. 286). Yet the positive part of the philosophy of the Laṅkāvatāra consists in the fact that it considers all ontological notions, such as being, non-being, cause, effect, etc., to be as much a manifestation in consciousness (*prajñaptimātra*) as the data of our senses or memory images to which they are applied. With Nāgārjuna, however, the emphasis was on the negative side. He regarded all things as having no essence; all things are in themselves self-contradictory, and whatever is self-contradictory is essenceless. According to the Laṅkāvatāra, however, the question whether anything is positive or negative, or whether anything has essence or not, or whether anything is caused or not, is invalid, for these notions are as much appearances in consciousness as those which were regarded as being their contents. It is, therefore, a false habit of ours that we make a division of some entities as being of the nature of contents or substance and others to be their qualities or logical relations. It is on account of this false habit that such questions can at all arise. In the proper perspective, however, it would be wrong to ask such questions as "What is real or what is unreal, what is positive, what is negative, what is cause, what is effect, what is reality, what is illusion or whether illusion ultimately exists or not?" For these imply an illegitimate connection of contents with relations. The mode of thinking that all contents have to be grasped by the various ontological or logical categories is wrong. It is, therefore, not possible for anyone to ask the philosopher in the Laṅkāvatāra, "How is experience possible, or what is the origin of the diverse phenomena, or how the diverse phenomena come into being?" for this implies the old fallacy of philosophies in general which the Laṅkāvatāra wishes to demolish. But it seems, however, that there is scope for asking such a question in the philosophy of Aśvaghosha, for there one ultimate reality is admitted, and it is said that out of that ultimate reality through the influence of ignorance the subjective mind manifested itself. Yet the avidyā is not regarded there as a dynamic power existing in the ultimate reality, which can be distinguished in its operation as a mode of activity which has its being in the ultimate reality, for the ultimate reality is pure self-identity. Thus the avidyā is regarded as the cause of the origin of the subjective mind and its development as a projection of an objective world from the mental states, yet it is regarded as being identical in essence with the ultimate reality, and the question remains unanswered, How is the notion of avidyā derived from that of the ultimate reality? It will be seen in our later chapters that in treating the relation of avidyā with Brahman the Vedāntists of the school of Śaṅkara expose themselves to the same difficulties which can be charged against Aśvaghosha. The fundamental fallacy of the philosophy of Aśvaghosha consists in the fact that it has run absolutely bankrupt, and in the name of explaining our experience it explains nothing and leaves it suspended in the air.

Chapter V

BUDDHIST IDEALISM (*continued*)

1. One of the fundamental tenets of idealism is the denial of relations. Thus Bradley, in arguing that if there are relations there must be qualities between which they are held, says that the situation of relations with regard to qualities is incomprehensible. If the relation is nothing to the qualities, then they are not related at all, and if so, they cease to be qualities and their relation is non-entity. But if it is something to them, then clearly that would require a new communicating relation. The relation cannot be an adjective to one or both of the terms, being something itself, if it does not bear a relation to the terms, how can it at all be anything to them? The introduction of a separate relation to relate the relations would land us in infinite regress. In this way it is difficult to determine how relations can stand towards the qualities which they are supposed to relate. Bradley's logic ultimately ends in the denial of all relations and in the affirmation of the one single, indivisible, timeless, real absolute; and the philosophy of Aśvaghosha reminds us of such an absolute wherein all distinctions have vanished, which does not consist of soul or thought or will but which at the same time forms the internal essence of them all in their non-distinctive and identical character. What this absolute is would always remain absolutely unpredicable, and this is true both in Aśvaghosha and in Bradley. According to Bradley all distinctions and relations are due to our partial view of things, and according to Aśvaghosha these are due to our particularising consciousness. Bradley has not sought to explain how these differences and partial

characters at all arise from the absolute, but Aśvaghosha has tried to give an explanation of these and has got into trouble. Aśvaghosha does not seem to trouble himself with Nāgārjuna's dialectic that all categories and relations are in themselves self-contradictory, and in this he also differs from Bradley, whose dialectical criticisms are but a repetition of Nāgārjuna after 2000 years. But the Laṅkāvatāra has a peculiar view of relations, namely, that relations are separate entities having the same character as the entities which they are supposed to relate, and it thus propounds the view that it is this attitude of mind which always tends to view all things in a relational order, and it is through this that the so-called relations attain their relating capacity. If relations can be taken in their separate character, standing like entities by the side of other entities, then that would destroy the very nature of relations. Here we have, therefore, a novel method of the refutation of relations based upon the demonstration of their inherent self-contradiction. Following this argument the Laṅkāvatāra does not find any reason why any absolute should be accepted to be real. The concept of reality has no meaning in itself; it is only a mental category which we try to apply to other entities when we call them real. Thus the denial of relations leads to the acceptance of the absolute in Aśvaghosha and Bradley, whereas in the Laṅkāvatāra this denial leads to the view that all phenomena are simply as they are and that all propositions are false. Relations are not reduced to qualities nor qualities to relations; neither are the qualities reduced to substance nor substance to qualities, but each is regarded as a separate appearance, and the root of all trouble is supposed to be in our modes of thinking, which makes a fusion of them all. If that is so, thought itself is an error, and neither thought nor perception is in any way further predicable or demonstrable than its appearances.

2. I must now turn to the other form of absolutism which was originally started by Maitreya and Asaṅga, and was elaborated by their disciple Vasubandhu. According to Vasubandhu all appearances are but transformations of the principle of consciousness by its inherent movement, and none of our cognitions is produced by any external objects which to us seem to be existing outside of us and generating our ideas. Just as in dreams one experiences different objects in different places and times without there being any real existence of them in those forms, places or times, or as in dreams many people are dreamt of as coming together and performing various actions, so what seems to be a real world of facts and external objects may well be explained as creations of the principle of intelligence. All that we know as subjective or objective are mere transformations of knowledge, and their essential reality is to be sought in their intrinsic nature as pure knowledge. All the diversity and the multiplicity of the world, having no substantial nature or reality in their apparent aspects as materiality, should be regarded as false. They are all but transformations of pure knowledge in their essential nature, and reality is that in which they are all true and real. The perceptual evidence of the existence of the objective world of matter cannot be trusted. Taking visual perception as an example, we may ask ourselves if the objects of the visual perception are one as a whole or many as atoms. They cannot be mere wholes, for whole would imply parts; they cannot be of the nature of atoms, for such atoms are not separately perceived; they cannot be of the nature of the component of atoms, for then the existence of the atoms cannot be proved. If the six atoms combine with one another it implies that the atoms have forms, for if the six atoms combine with one another in one identical point it would mean that the combined group would not have its collection bigger

than that of an atom and would therefore be invisible. Again, if the objects of awareness and perception were only wholes, then succession and sequence would be inexplicable and our perception of separate and distinct things would remain unaccountable. So, though they have no real objective existence, yet perception leads us to believe that they have such existence. In the experience of the world of objects we are dreaming under the influence of the instinctive roots of a beginningless habit of a false imaginative construction, and in our dreams we construct the objective world. It is only when we become awake with the transcendent knowledge of oneness of all things that we find the world construction to be as false as the dream construction of diverse appearances.

3. It is true that we ordinarily distinguish between two modes of knowledge, viz. perception and memory. In perception we feel that objects are before us, whereas in memory we feel that we are remembering things which were known to us before, but which are not now present before us. But on the analogy of dreams it is possible to suppose that there may be knowledge of things without there being actually the objects presented before us. But an objection may still be raised: "What constitutes, then, the difference between our two modes of knowledge as perception and memory?" To this Vasubandhu's answer is that perception is a special mode of the self-creation of knowledge, such that when the thought is manifesting itself in that particular mode it is called perception, and it is only by depending on such modes of self-creation of thought that memory is possible. What Vasubandhu means by this is that our perceptual form of cognition is one particular mode of self-creation of thought in which objects are felt to be presented before us; whereas memory represents another mode of the self-creation of thought,

which is dependent on the process of the perceptual mode of self-creation, such that only those objects, which were presented to us by the activity of that mode, could be presented to us in the form of memory, with this peculiar characteristic that here things are not felt to be presented to us but as having been presented to us before and already acquired and conserved in the mind. Now another objection may be raised, that if each series of thoughts is produced in each particular centre, each series being independent and separate from the other series, what is it that would regulate the law and order of thought? If in each centre particular series of ideas are spun out, then there would be no way by which the uniformity of experience or intercourse between various persons, and the uniform results that are attained, could be explained. To this Vasubandhu's answer is that though it may be admitted that the different series of thoughts and ideas are each limited to themselves separately, yet the different series of thoughts and ideas may be supposed to be influencing one another. Thus, instead of admitting the intercourse between one mind and another through the means of an objective material world, the series of thoughts in different individuals may be regarded as having an intercourse between them directly through their own specific experiences. Thus the idea of murdering one's enemy may be of such a type that it will produce in one a sensation of the continuity of his thought processes, and produce such other impressions of bodily injury in the injured person and in other individuals that they would consider the man to be a murderer, though actually there may not be any physical body which has been actually decapitated in the materialistic fashion. The nature of the transformation in the self-creation of thought is more clearly explained in Vasubandhu's Triṃśikā. There it is said that a power only transforms itself on one side as the various selves and the categories of relations and the like, and on the other hand as the objective world in the form of colour, sound, taste, etc. The meaning of transformation is production of effect, different from that of the causal movement simultaneously at the time of the cessation of the causal moment. So on account of such a transformation of the self-evolving thought there is, on the one hand, the notion of the different perceivers, and, on the other hand, that of the things perceived as outside of them. But since this transformation is a transformation of self-evolving thought, there cannot be anything like outside or inside; yet such is the mode of the transformation that each individual self seems to perceive an objective world before it. It may be noted in this connection that the transformation of the self-evolving thought that is here admitted is regarded as real transformation, and it is in this sense different from the illusory transformation through ignorance admitted by Aśvaghosha. But this does not mean that the knowables are existing as they are known. It merely means that the ground of transformation, the *vijñāna* or consciousness, exists; for there can neither be any transformation nor any illusory imposition without there being any ground. The transformation of consciousness means that there are no external objects, but there are only the transformations of consciousness in the form of knowable objects.

4. The mode of causation here accepted is that of pratītyasamutpāda, as in all Buddhist theories; and *pratītyasamutpāda* here means the rise of the effect which is different from the causal moment and which is simultaneous with the cessation of the causal moment. There is thus the consciousness as the ground which appears transformed as knowable objects, and there is no excitant outside it in the objective world which may be regarded as having caused the transformation of the

consciousness. The nature of this transformation is different from the notion of transformation with which we are familiar in the Sāṃkhya. In the Sāṃkhya, transformation or *pariṇāma* means that all the diverse transformatory products or effects were already existent in the ground cause, and the causal movement of transformation only revealed those which were lying hidden in it. But here the transformation means that on account of the various root-instincts and the notions of self, and other psychological entities as well as the root-instincts of perceiving other objective entities such as colour, sound, etc., these notions of self and subjectivity and the objective colour, form, etc. have come into being, though these cannot be regarded as the transformation in any real sense like that of the Sāṃkhya. The transformation only means that at its first moment the causal entity which remained as such appeared as the effect-entity simultaneously with the cessation of the first moment. It cannot therefore be said that the elements that constitute the effect-entity were already existent in the causal entity, and therefore when particular effect-entities are supplanted by other entities it cannot also be said that the same were either produced or destroyed. What we have in this transformation is that different moments are characterised by different characters which are called the effects. That being so, nothing further can be said about the effect-characters than that they had risen into appearance and disappeared. The only fundamental element behind them as the ground was the consciousness. The argument is put forward by some people that unless there were at least two permanent entities behind the two permanent appearances, viz. subject and object, it would not be possible even illusorily to relate the one with the other, and hence it would be wrong to say that non-existent qualities or characters are being affirmed and that such affirmation constitutes the nature of the world-process. But this is indefensible, because even with the acceptance of two entities and their characters such illusory misaffirmations would be unjustifiable; for the Buddhists deny the notion of class-concepts and, that being denied, each specific quality would belong to that individual and it would be impossible to affirm that quality of any other entity. Again, it would be impossible to affirm the existence of any entity apart from its cognisance in knowledge. The affirmation of qualities, again, can have reference only to the affirmation of cognitional characters and not to the affirmation of characters in themselves. Therefore, since everything has a reference only to what is felt in knowledge, the requirement of the existence of separate entities or characters in themselves for explaining wrong affirmations cannot be defended.

5. This transformation is primarily of two kinds, viz. change of the nature of the *ālayavijñāna* or the transforming consciousness, and change that is effected in consequence thereof. The first change in the ālayavijñāna consists in the accumulation of the results of the infinite root-instincts. The second change is of two kinds, as affirmation of psychosis and as the perceptive character. Of these the first is called *vipāka* and the other two are called *manana* and *vishayavijñapti*. The ālayavijñāna is called *ālaya* because it is the home of all the seeds or roots of those instincts that lead to world-experiences. This ālayavijñāna seems to manifest itself in two forms: as the consciousness of inner psychological stages forming the psychosis or the microcosm, and externally as the limitless, unoccupied and occupied space. The internal microcosm consists of the root-tendencies of the affirmation of diverse characters and relations of sense-qualities, class characters and names. These, however, remain in the ālayavijñāna in an undifferentiated manner, and their specific characters do not exist there in their distinguishable and separable forms. Since all these elements, which constitute subjectivity and externality, are existent in the ālayavijñāna, it has to be regarded as a concrete universe, though it is impossible to ascribe any specific or distinguishable character to it. Thus in the ālayavijñāna we have touch, feelings, attention, discrimination associated with names and volition. The word contact (*sparśa*) is a special term which means pleasure or pain arising out of the threefold associations of sense-object and sense-knowledge. The sense, again, means that special way or mode in which the specific sense-pleasure is experienced in association with sense-knowledge. This word also means the notion that is associated with sense-knowledge that sense was in contact with an object. Attention (*manaskāra*) means that by which the mind is directed and kept steady in its object. The term feeling (*vedanā*) signifies the positive, i.e. pleasurable, the negative, i.e. sorrowful, and the indifferent which is neither pleasurable nor painful. The term discrimination (*vivecanā*) means the function by which one differentiates two sense-characters, the blue and the yellow. The term volition (*cetanā*) means the effort of the mind by which the mind is drawn to different objects just as iron filings are attracted by magnets. When it is said that the ālayavijñāna contains feeling, that feeling is, of course, neither pleasure nor pain but a feeling on the level of indifference; and the contact (sparśa), which is said to be inherent in the ālayavijñāna, as also the other elements such as effort, discrimination, attention, etc., also exist in an undifferentiated state. This ālayavijñāna is not one self-identical entity, but it is always splitting itself up like currents and waves so that the effects, that are produced out of it, react against it; and they are also reacted upon by the instinctive roots contained in it or such instinctive roots as newly accumulate through these effects.

This also explains the fact how one ālayavijñāna expresses itself in diverse individual centres. And in the case of the individual current or wave, representing a particular individual centre which has attained right wisdom and has become an *arhat*, the ālayavijñāna ceases to exist, for such a wave becomes cut asunder from it, and lost in the underlying consciousness. All thoughts of the internal psychosis, together with all associations of morality and immorality, either potential or actual, are held in the ālayavijñāna.

6. The third transformation of the ālayavijñāna is in the form of perception of objects of six kinds, viz. colour, sound, smell, taste, touch, mental entities, and these may be either moral, immoral or indifferent. It comes, therefore, that all the sense knowledge, ideas and thoughts, rise into appearance in accordance with the necessity involved in their anterior antecedent moments. Just as in a big volume of flowing water there may be one wave or more in accordance with the specific causes that are associated with one or more of such waves, and yet the volume of water may remain the same throughout, so from the ālayavijñāna there may be one or more cognitions, while the ālayavijñāna may all the time be flowing in its own course. All that appear as cognitions are non-existent as independent entities, and are only impositions on the nature of consciousness (*abhūtaparikalpa*); there is not the slightest reason to think that cognitions have existence outside themselves and outside their ground, viz. the ālayavijñāna. If the ālayavijñāna is called the depository of all seeds, it is due to the fact that it has the power of producing all kinds of diverse cognitional creations. It has already been pointed out that as the ālayavijñāna may be said to create as its effect the various experiences, so the experiences also in their turn may be regarded as determining the future activity of the ālayavijñāna. So all the movement of the ālayavijñāna is due to the mutual action and reaction carried on from beginningless time between the ālayavijñāna and its creations, and it is by this mutual action and reaction that the ālayavijñāna continues to create all cognitional appearances that constitute the world-process. The most important point to be noted in this connection is that the ālayavijñāna is not a differenceless entity as was conceived by Aśvaghosha in the Śraddhotpādasūtra, but it is the concrete universality which contains within itself all the potencies and roots of all psychical states, as also the objective space-consciousness. In one sense, therefore, it may be thought that this system presents a theory in which thought itself is somehow externalised in the form of objects that are perceived. The objects that are perceived have no real existence in their independent nature as material objects, but their reality consists in the nature of consciousness; as such they have been projected in a form of externality from the ālayavijñāna, which contains roots or germs that can explain the fact of such a projection from the ālayavijñāna in the form of diverse appearances that constitute our phenomenal world. The question of the dynamic power by which the ālayavijñāna can be conceived as split up into subjective and objective order is explained in this system by the supposition that in a beginningless series creations are emanating from the ālayavijñāna, and such creations are again reacting upon it; and it is by this mutual action and reaction, reflection and re-reflection, that intercourse between the physical and mental world and *vice versa* is made possible. The cognitional forms that are supposed to be created have, of course, no further reality than their mere appearances, because they pass on in a series like waves from a volume of water flowing in diverse currents; but though they are metaphysically indeterminable yet they have sufficient substantiality to carry on our world-process, for all entities are indeterminable in their own nature and are only predicable so far as they are knowable. The three kinds of essencelessness of these appearances consist in the fact that they are indefinable, that no essence can be described as the nature of their sources and that being permanent they have no nature. All things and characters that appear before us are mere illusory impositions and are relative in their nature, and as such they can neither be said to be existent nor non-existent. Their characters consist merely of their appearances and therefore, since they have no nature of their own, they are essenceless in their nature. Again, these characters simply appear on the cessation of other characters and therefore, though they may be supposed to be originating from somewhere, there is really no cause from which they originate. They are, therefore, in their ultimate nature nothing else but the ultimate entity from which they seem to appear.

7. The question now is, what is the nature of the ālayavijñāna? The ālayavijñāna, as has already been pointed out, has to be admitted as the ground of all individual centres of experience. It is in it that the experiences that are passed and gone in any particular centre or individual are conserved and synthesised, for we know that since the Buddhists do not admit any permanent soul or mind it would be difficult to explain how the past experiences of any individual are related to or influence the future experiences of the same individual. The pure consciousness, which is absolutely differenceless and absolutely devoid of all potencies or tendencies, would hardly be able to explain the synthesis that is required in experience which involves action and reaction of past experience and past tendencies against the present experiences. It is for this reason that the ālayavijñāna has to be admitted as a hypothesis to explain the possi-

bility of experience. It is like the *buddhitattva* of the Sāṃkhya, which is knotted all over with the resultants of all past experiences in the form of instinctive roots, and in the ground of which all synthesis of new sensations or relations as new impositions can take place. The ālayavijñāna is one, but it holds within it all the instinctive tendencies which make the appearance of diverse individual subjects and their experiences possible, for all notions of diverse subjects, diverse objects and diverse cognitions arise out of it as its pulsations. It is out of this that the notion of diverse individual subjects springs together with the notions of sensations, thoughts, and the diverse relations, as also the space-consciousness associated with them. The world outside is not like petrified intelligence, but it is our awareness which has diverse forms and which thus appears as external objects. Our inner experience is thus limited to thought, and the diverse thoughts, sensations or relations cannot be regarded as having any further existence than mere essenceless appearance, and ālayavijñāna is a ground in which these are harmonised and ordered with reference to individual subjects (which are in themselves but impositions) which also arise out of it; it is through this continual reflection and re-reflection, action and reaction, between the conserved elements of the ālayavijñāna and the newer impositions that arise out of it, that our experiential process can be explained. Even as such the ālayavijñāna is only a hypothetical state without which the experiential order cannot be explained; but what is the ground of this ālayavijñāna?

8. As a ground of this ālayavijñāna we have the pure consciousness called the *vijñaptimātra*, which is beyond all experiences, transcendent and pure consciousness, pure bliss, eternal, unchangeable and unthinkable. It is this one pure being as pure consciousness and pure bliss, eternal and unchangeable like the Brahman of the

Vedānta, that forms the ultimate ground and ultimate essence of all appearance; even the ālayavijñāna is an imposition of it, as are all the different states of it which make the world-order possible. The nature of this ultimate pure consciousness is absolutely indeterminable and unthinkable and it has no object whatsoever. Even the knowledge that the ultimate reality is this pure consciousness is a false imposition. At the time of emancipation a particular series of tendencies and creations associated with a particular subjective centre ceases, and as a result thereof the ālayavijñāna ceases to have any activity of any kind with reference to such a subjective centre; this can only happen when all other tendencies of the subjective centre and all characters and appearances associated with it are ultimately merged in this pure consciousness. Thus we see that the ultimate reality is one, being self-identical, pure consciousness and pure bliss, which is thus different from the Tathatā of Aśvaghosha and very similar to the Brahman of the Upanishads. It is from this interfunctioning of avidyā or ignorance that there arises the cosmic consciousness of ālayavijñāna, which contains within it the seed-potentialities of all notions representing subjective centres, objects and their cognitions and thoughts. On the ground of the ālayavijñāna cognitional forms are synthesised with particular subjective centres and their works in a spatio-temporal order, and in this sense the ālayavijñāna may be regarded as the universal repository of all subjects and their experiences. Those who are familiar with the doctrine of the Upanishads and their later interpretations by Śaṅkara and other writers will see to what extent this doctrine resembles the Vedāntic theory. All characters, entities and individuals are as much illusory here as in the Vedānta. It is only with reference to the transformation of the ālayavijñāna into the various notions and states that arise from it that there is some difference, but, ultimately speaking, the ālayavijñāna is only a hypothetical state which may be regarded as much an imposition on the pure consciousness and as much false as are the ordinary experiences. The ālayavijñāna is only a relative relation, an element as compared with the individual experiences. All impositions are regarded as *abhūtaparikalpa* or imposition of that which never was. But how are these impositions possible? To this we have the old answer of a beginningless action and reaction between accumulated potencies and new acquirements due to them. The formation of the new acquirements or the new experiences are regarded as states which are produced as modificatory characters of the different moments of the ālayavijñāna in a particular mode and with reference to a particular subjective centre. The external world of matter is thus false, and the wave in our experience is but knowledge appearing in diverse functions as purely internal and temporal and also as external, temporal and spatial.

9. Vasubandhu cannot be regarded as the originator of this particular type of idealism. A recently discovered manuscript of Madhyantavibhaṅga by Maitreya, which was elaborated by Asaṅga and commented upon by Vasubandhu and Sthiramati, gives a form of idealism which is very nearly the same as that propounded by Vasubandhu himself in his Viṃśikā and Triṃśikā. It is said there that neither the appearance of objects has any objective reality nor has the notion of self any subjective nucleus; the appearance of objectivity and subjectivity is therefore false. One reason that is offered for this falsehood is that in all cognitional modes existence and character appear to be identified, or rather existences are supposed to have characters or characters to be existential. Since existence as such is different from character, the attribution of the one to the

other must necessarily be false. This indeed is a reversion to the logic of the Laṅkāvatāra, where relations and characters are definitely regarded as having the same status as being and as such, since neither of them can be regarded as primary, the affirmation of characters regarding being would be false. In this treatise two opposite arguments are discussed; one argument is that since our perceptions are false, therefore there are no external realities as the objective basis of such perception. The other argument is that our perceptions are false because they are of the same form as the objects, and it is the latter which is supported by Maitreya and his commentators. It is again and again repeated that the vijñāna or cognition is *abhinnarūpa*, i.e. of the identical form as the objects. This, however, does not mean that the external world is petrified intelligence. But it only means that the forms of objects are but forms of cognition, as in Vasubandhu, where, also, we find that the series of cognitions in each particular centre is determined by the instinctive roots that are present as determining factors of that particular series. The falsehood consists in the fact that there are no objects and yet the notions of subjects and cognitions manufacture the so-called objective reality; another interesting suggestion that is found in it is that the falsehood is due to the fact that the objects may not be such as are represented by the cognitions (*yathā vijñāna vijñānanarthaḥ parikalpyate tathārthasyabhāvo*). Since each cognition in its own turn is determined by other cognitions, each cognition is false in its own nature. It is for this reason that not only the objects represented by cognitions are false but also the subject or the perceiver represented by them is false, and since both the subject and the object are false the cognition itself becomes false. But though it is not possible to affirm any reality of anything, yet it is also not possible to say that there is any pure negation, for there is at least the illusion (*bhrāntimātrotpādāt sarvathābhāvo'pi na*). It is not possible to enter into any discussion regarding this illusory appearance, for it transcends all objects and all logical dialectics. If there was absolute negation, then there would be no bondage and no emancipation and there would be no necessity for any philosophy.

10. All appearances have three forms. In one form appearance may be regarded as mere illusory imposition (*parikalpita*); in another form it may be regarded as having only a relative reality on which our worldly intercourse is based (*paratantra*); in another form it affirms that character of the appearance by which it can neither be said to be existent nor non-existent in its own changeless nature. But here also, apart from the various cognitions which are the forms of the objects they represent, it is admitted that there is one pure consciousness which is absolutely eternal, and it is by entrance into this that the final emancipation is achieved. Let us now turn to the Buddhist doctrine of causation in the Theravāda and the Mahāyāna.

11. Mrs Rhys Davids has pointed out that the word *paccaya* is nearly parallel to the English word "relation". The commentators say that paccaya means "cause of what it makes to come". This second meaning of course reduces paccaya to the merely causal relation whereas paccaya as such etymologically ought to mean "relation in general". There is also another word which has more or less the same significance as paccaya, namely, the word *paṭṭhāna*. The word paccaya is generally reserved for such causal conditions as can introduce some energy towards either the production or the specific nature of the effect. This implies that the paccaya has a particular energy or *śakti* which is transmitted to the effect-entity. In a later work of the Theravāda school (*abhidhammāttha saṇgaha*) twenty-four different kinds of the paṭṭhāna or correlation are enumerated, such as (1) condition (*hetu*), which is generally reserved for the six moral roots of a person's character such as attachment, ignorance, etc.; (2) object, such as the object of consciousness of the five senses and manas; (3) dominance, such as volitional energy, intention and the like; (4) and (5) contiguity, immediate or mediate, such as succession of mental states; (6) co-existence, which means simultaneous production; (7) reciprocity, which means mutual relation; (8) and (9) dependence and sufficing condition, meaning a group of effective conditions which can immediately produce a result; (10) antecedence; (11) consequence; (12) habitual recurrence; (13) deeds, which are the intermediate link between the will and result; (14) result; (15) mental or material support or nutriment; (16) mental or psychophysical control; (17) concentration; (18) a course of action leading to a result; (19) association; (20) dissociation; (21) presence; (22) and (23) negation; (24) continuance. (Rhys Davids' article on Buddhist Relations, *E.R.E.*) This account is based on the Paṭṭhāna and Abhidhammāttha and Ledi Sadaw's article on Buddhist Theory. In the Śālistambhasūtra, the theory of pratītyasamutpāda is described as twofold in nature, that due to *hetus* and that due to *pratyayas*. The one due to pratyayas is that kind of causality where the effect-entity follows the causal entity without there being any notion of the one cause consciously producing the other. Thus from the seed there is the shoot, the leaf and so forth. That due to hetu is regarded as that in which the constituting elements produce the diverse kinds of functions or qualities in the effect-entity, though none of the constituent elements have any notion in them that they are producing similar qualities in the effect-entity. Thus the earth-element gives the hardness to the seed, the water-element the water consistency, the fire-element its heat, the *ākāśa*-element its porosity, and so forth; but yet it should not be thought that the seed was different from the shoot, or that the seed was the same as the shoot, or that the seed was destroyed and at the same time the shoot was produced, or that it was from the destroyed shoot that the seed was produced, or that it was from the undestroyed seed that the shoot was produced. The whole point is that the seed is destroyed and simultaneously with it the shoot is produced, just as when one scale point goes down the other rises up; but yet it is seen that if the cause is sufficient it produces the effect and that the effect is also somehow similar to the cause. It is summarily described in this way that the pratītya-samutpāda has five aspects, namely, that it is not to be viewed either from the point of view of the effect being a transformation of the cause (*na śāśvatahetuto*), or that it is produced out of destruction of the cause (*nochhedahetuto*), or that the effect and the cause are not identical (*na śaṅkrāntahetuto*), but that the effect follows from a sufficient cause (*paritta hetuto*) and that the effect is somehow similar to the cause (*tatsadṛśānuprabandhatas*). The Śālistambhasūtra thus admits that in effect-complexes the effect elements correspond to the causal elements in the causal complexes, but the idea of the transmission of energy from the causal entities and causal complexes to the effect-entities or effect-complexes is wholly denied. According to it, it cannot also be said that there are abiding relations between the causal complex and the effect-complex, such that the effect-complex may be regarded as a transformation of the causal complex or identical with it in nature, or that the destruction of the causal complex is also generative of the effect-complex, but we have simply the fact that the effect-complex is neither one with nor different from the causal complex and that simultaneously with the cessation of the causal complex the effect-complex springs up. This does away with the idea that relations exist permanently whether relating entities exist or not, and in the Laṅkāvatāra we have noticed that relations are also regarded as being entities of the same kind that are to be related, and so much so that it becomes impossible to associate any relations with the relationable entities and thus all entities being unrelationable become unspeakable and indefinable.

12. According to Candrakīrti's interpretation of Nāgārjuna's Kārikā we find that things are produced only in relation to or with reference to other entities which are regarded as causes. Nothing further can be said as to what is meant by "in relation to". It is said also that such a phrase as "things are produced only relatively to their causes" ultimately means that things are neither produced without a cause, nor by one cause, nor with many causes, nor out of themselves, nor out of others, nor conjointly out of their own association with others, but that things are mere appearances as they are shown in ordinary experience. Causality in this sense is not a real relation but only a relative appearance. In chapter 14 of Nāgārjuna's work the notion of relation is definitely refuted. It is said that neither cognition, nor the sense-organs, nor their objects, can have any dual or triple relation because relation presupposes others, and the notion of otherness is itself false. Thus we see a table is a table with reference to a chair, but without making any reference to any other entity no entity is intelligible by itself. That being so, every entity involves all other entities for its own support. If the chair and the table were entirely different it would not be necessary that a table should be a table because of its relation to the chair. Moreover, the category of otherness cannot be supposed to belong to any entity by virtue of itself, its appearance is only for explaining our ordinary experience which is based on false notions. So it follows that if there is no otherness there is nothing also which can be designated as the other. So in the case of the cognitive relation, since there is no otherness in either the subject or the object, nor can each one of them be regarded as the other *per se*, there cannot be any relation between them. If difference between them were real and other with reference to the others, then there would be no way of relating them. If they are all identical, then also there would be no relation. If the three terms of the cognitive relation are identical with one another, then also there cannot be a relation. Since in the absence of otherness or of "others" there cannot be any relation, there cannot also be related entities.

13. With regard to specific relations also, apart from the elaborate refutations of Nāgārjuna we have further refutations of a more or less different nature from Śāntarakshita and Kamalaśīla. Thus they hold that the Buddhists do not believe in any qualities, so that a qualified being as such would be false. The objects that are perceived are merely entities and are not associated with any kind of characters outside of them. The question may arise, "How then can one explain the category of difference or how can one explain the apprehension of things as being associated with other characters as when it is said, 'this is a qualified thing or this is its special character'?" In answer to such an objection it is urged that a special character of a thing is merely its difference from others, but it does not establish any qualified character and the difference itself again is not separate from entities that are differentiated. It is only an entity that is regarded as different in its aspects as negating other entities. It is not true that in perceiving an object we perceive it also as different. When any entity is perceived as apart from all other objects and its unique nature is so grasped, it is only then that it is said to be different in linguistic usage. So the category of difference is never perceived either as an entity or as the different object which are contrasted with one another, but it is only a mental mode which has never come to us directly in perception. Speaking of universals they say that they may be of two kinds: firstly, those which are unassociated with any relation or reference to other individuals, and secondly, those that are intimately related to different individuals. That which is not related to any individuals is, as such, formless and may be accepted as such, but that which is related to individuals has its universality defined only by a reference to certain individuals. For if the class-concepts or universals do not negate the individuals that come under them they would not be class-concepts at all. So such class-concepts or universals can only be grasped in relation with specific individuals whom they are negating. There are no universals which can be apprehended by themselves, and the apprehension of the so-called class-concepts is nothing more than the apprehension of the different individuals in which their constituent specific characters are ignored. In this view there are no abstract general concepts, it is only the individuals that stand as universals and only their specific individual characters are for the time being wiped out of the mind (compare Berkeley's *Theory of Abstract Universals*). It is said by the opponents of the Buddhists that all universals are permeated by the specific characters and, if this is so, then the universal characters and the individual characters could not be in any way differentiated and neither the one nor the other could be recognised. Again, since there are no other categories of difference apart from individuals with which they are falsely associated, and since the class-concepts cannot touch any of these individuals, the idea suggested about the class-concepts, as being nothing but individuals which stand for the universals with their individual peculiarities ignored, would be wrong. If, however, it is held that the class-concepts are associated with the individuals having specific characters, then the notion of class-concepts would apply to individuals with specific characters, which is not admitted by anybody. If it is held that the class-concepts are indescribable in themselves and yet they may be applied to individuals, then there will be such distinction within the class-concepts, by virtue of which it should be possible to apply them to different individuals, and in that case the class-concepts themselves would have concrete characters. If such specific character be denied to the class-concepts, then they will be like pure negations, for if they are nothing, then they cannot have any similarity with anything else. For they have no character and yet they have special functions, they must at least be substances, for that cannot be anything which has a function and yet is not a substantial entity. If it is a substantial entity, then it becomes an individual. And these class-concepts cannot be regarded as having any specific characters, for even if these specific characters are to be from purely non-existing things like the hare's horn, then that would also make the class-concepts individuals. In reality the Buddhists denied also negation as "otherness", for this negation is nothing else than the mere fact that one entity is not another.

14. The idea, therefore, is that in perception one only perceives a unique, indescribable something and then associates it with relations of quality, quantity, universality and particularity, and the like, which are all false and groundless. The datum of perception is thus absolutely characterless, unspeakable and undefinable. But now the question arises that if the datum of a perception be indeterminable, how is it possible for us to be associated with diverse determinable relations? And the Buddhist's answer is that though this knowledge as perceptual datum is indeterminable in itself, yet it has the power of associating with it diverse relations of quality, quantity, etc. It should, on no account, be thought that these perceptual data are in themselves without any determinatory nature or character. But, on the other hand, they have the fullest determination in themselves of such a nature as in themselves they stand as differentiated from other entities of different characters, and as also assimilable to such other entities having like characters. When the Buddhist says that they are indeterminable, what is meant is only that no conscious process of assimilation, discrimination or association of diverse kinds has taken place. The perceptual data in themselves are of a very varied nature, and it is on account of this varied nature of theirs that they have in themselves the power by which different kinds of relations are associated with them, which transforms them into the varied forms of determinate perception. Thus, when it is said that perception only reveals the entities in their unique nature, it does not mean that their nature is unknowable or indeterminable; on the other hand, they are sufficiently knowable and determinable, and their indeterminateness consists only in the fact that the process of a determination involving the application of the diverse categories of relation is not a perceptual event but a post-perceptual operation, and should therefore be excluded from the sphere of perception itself. The difference of Buddhism from other realistic systems, such as the Nyāya and the Vaiśeshika, consists in the fact that in these systems perception is drawn out into a long affair, which includes not only the perceptual datum but other subsequent application of categories and association of relations, until the perception takes an articulated form as "this is fire". The Buddhist, however, rests contented only with the perceptual datum which he calls perception, as separated from the association of other categories and relations arising out of the necessity of those perceptual data, as being entirely external to them, and therefore not given to the senses and only applied through the imaginative tendencies of the mind (Tattvasaṃgraha, p. 390).

15. Śāntarakshita so much emphasises the independent and valid nature of the perceptual data, that in defining perception he not only introduces the qualification that they should be only such data as are given to the senses previous to the application of the categories of relation (following Diṅnāga), but they should also be unerring (*abhrānta*). It is evident that it is not possible for anyone to say whether any perceptual datum is erroneous or not before the application of the categories of relations, but yet he thought that the definition of perception should contain this qualification to distinguish the erroneous perceptual data from the right ones. This means that according to Śāntarakshita and many of his later followers perceptual data (which according to the Buddhist idealists are always mental), having in themselves their unique characters, contained in them such distinctions of validity or invalidity as would render them so apprehended at a later stage, when the categories of relations would be applied to them by virtue of the necessity of their own unique natures. The nature of validity or invalidity, which, of course, is determinable only at a later stage after the application of the categories, is determined by the uncontradicted testimony of the different senses or through their contradiction. In the case of the idealistic Buddhists, who do not admit any external object, this would amount to self-coherence or incoherence as compared with later experiences. In the idealistic Buddhism, as explained by Śāntarakshita, the cognitions are of the form of objects; that is, our awarenesses are of the forms of blue or yellow and it is in accordance with such type of diverse awarenesses that we project the blue or the yellow as the objects outside the knowledge and say that we have the awareness of the yellow or the blue. The process of knowledge is not from object to cognition, but from cognition to object; not that the objects are produced by cognition, but they are simply regarded as existing in correspondence with the particular cognitions that refer to them. The cognitions that arise in the form of objects carry with them the impression that they are referring to certain objective entities corresponding to them, and this is called the cognitional activity or cognitional operation. The objects are not only invariably associated with the cognitions, but the cognitions also appear to be taken in the objects as representing the object-consciousness. It is this special function that is meant by the phrase that the cognition has an intercourse with the object (*arthaprāpaṇa vyāpāra*). We start with different awarenesses having the form of different objects, and these object-form-awarenesses carry with them the projection by which we feel as if there are certain objects to which these awarenesses are referred, and it is this objective reference of subjective object-form-awareness that may be regarded as the cognising activity in our intercourse with the so-called external world through knowledge. Particular kinds of object-form-awarenesses fill our minds with particular emotions and desires and lead us to other kinds of consciousness of activity, leading further to other kinds of object-form-cognitions.

16. In trying to refute the existence of external objects Śāntarakshita proceeds to refute the atomic doctrine, some slight suggestions regarding which have already been made in our examination of Vasubandhu's idealism. It may be pointed out in this connection that Śāntarakshita does not believe in the existence of an eternal principle of knowledge as *vijñaptimātratā* as was believed by Vasubandhu. Thus in refuting the Upanishadic view he says that when we have cognitions of sound, colour, taste, etc. coming in a changing series, we cannot believe that there is a permanent principle of consciousness underlying them all. No one ever experiences the changing cognitions to be in the same state always; on the other hand we have now a colour sensation, then a sound sensation, then a taste sensation, and so on. If these were all but transformations or reflections or modifications of one eternal principle of consciousness, then they would have all appeared in one moment, for their underlying ground being always in an unchanged state there would be no reason why there should be a change in the cognitions which are based on this changeless ground. If the modifications are found to be always changing, then since their ground is identical with them, the ground itself would also be changed. Moreover, a permanent, unchanging pure consciousness is never revealed to us either in perception or by inference, for in our experience we always find the changing mental state, but we never find the unchanged consciousness. Had there been any such unchanging consciousness as a ground of all these changing states that also must have been experienced. In the view in which it is admitted that with reference to each subject there is a different series of cognitions, it can well be imagined that there may be bondage with reference to any particular series or emancipation with reference to another particular series; but in the view which holds that there is one eternal consciousness, it would be difficult to see how it can explain the different kinds of cognition or emancipation or bondage with reference to different individuals. If there is only one consciousness, and if that is made impure through ignorance, then there is no chance of any emancipation; or if this consciousness is pure, then there is no chance of any bondage. According to Sāntarakshita what we call an individual is but a definite and particular series of cognitive states arising in the appearance and being destroyed the next moment, so that the experience of each individual is limited to that particular series which refers to that particular individual and the sins or virtues of experience of any particular series is limited to itself. He does not deny that there may be intercourse between one series and another without any objective basis, but he does not believe in any permanent ground or entity as pure consciousness as Vasubandhu does, and holds that the infinite number of states and experiences occurring in any particular series has such a special relation with the preceding and succeeding members of that series that though these states are in themselves indefinable, they somehow peculiarly belong to that particular series.

17. We already know of an old discussion between the Vātsīputrīya sects of Buddhists and Vasubandhu on the nature of the existence of soul. The Vātsīputrīyas declared that some individual must necessarily exist, because there could not be spontaneous births, and according to them the individuals could not be regarded as being identical with the elements of a person or life. To this Vasubandhu's reply had been that the so-called entities have no reality as such, but they only appear to be so in knowledge (i.e. they are only *prajñaptisat* and not *svarūpasat*). Thus a glass may be regarded as one individual piece, but this is only an appearance when we know that there is no such whole as a glass, but there are only the combining elements, and the glass is but a name for the combining atoms. The Vātsīputrīyas, however, in answer try to maintain that the individual is neither one with the combining elements nor entirely different from them (see Stcherbatsky's translation of Abhidharmakośa, chap. 8). The Sammitīyas, who are a branch of the Vātsīputrīyas, also believe in the doctrine of *pudgala* or an individual entity, and they drew their inspiration from the Bhārahārasūtra (Saṃyutta 3. 25), in which it was said that the five physical and intellectual constituents formed the burden, and desire was the carrier of this burden, whereas there is an individual or the pudgala which carries the burden and this pudgala is described in the following words: "This is a monk, of such a name, of such a family, living on such food, etc."; but it is not clear from this passage whether the so-called pudgala or the individual is not itself a burden or is not itself being carried on by the fivefold constituents. The Sammitīyas are, however, very anxious to hold that there is an ego which holds the burden and the pudgalas; but though they admit the pudgalas as different, these are not non-different from the constituents; for without these Skandhas there is no pudgala, yet with these Skandhas there is a pudgala. Śāntarakshita, in refuting the Vātsīputrīya doctrine, says that to say that the pudgala is different from the constituent elements, and yet not different from them, is to say that it is illusory.

18. Kamalaśīla further adds that since the Vātsīputrīyas cannot give any particular character to this so-called pudgala it must be without any essence. Since, also, pudgala cannot be differentiated in any character from the fivefold constituents, it cannot be regarded as having any separate existence. The Vātsīputrīyas are unable to say whether the pudgalas are permanent or momentary, and they cannot also show their place in our worldly experience as associated with practical purposes. Thus the doctrine of the Vātsīputrīyas that there is an individual apart from the fivefold constituents is to be regarded as false. Other doctrines regarding the existence of a permanent soul have also been refuted by Śāntarakshita, the details of which may be omitted in our present treatment of this subject. The existence of the external world as a conglomeration of atoms is also refuted by Kamalaśīla and Śāntarakshita by exposing the contradictions that arise from such suppositions. That being so, and there being no external objects and there being no individual selves which perceive them, the conclusion to which Śāntarakshita and Kamalaśīla force us is that there are only the cognitions arising into appearance and disappearing the next moment without there being any other perceiver and the objects of perception. There are thus only parallel streams of different series of conscious states, and it is possible for the states of one conscious series to influence the states of another conscious series, each particular stream of the series of conscious states being popularly regarded as an individual. In these conscious streams there is neither any perceiver nor any perceived object, and the states are simply revealed as individual appearances. There is no idea of a cogniser or a cognising activity or a cognised object, for a conscious state is only one entity which cannot thus be divided in such threefold manner. If it is admitted that an external object exists apart from the object-form of awareness, it would be difficult to see how the phenomenon of cognition can be explained, because the objects being of an entirely different nature from cognition, there would be no way in which the cognition of the objects can be related. It is well known that our knowing an object cannot produce any change or modification in it. If that be so, how can it be argued that the object can produce a modification in our knowledge in generating a particular kind of cognition corresponding to that object? Again, it is wrong to suppose that in knowing a thing there is any cognitive activity, for knowing simply means the illumination or revelation of a particular objective form; that being so, what other activity can be imagined which would be necessary for the cognition of external objects? It cannot also be admitted that there can be any separate cognitional idea apart from the fact of perceiving the objects. If it is said that there is a consciousness as the unchanging ground of all particular cognitions, then there will be no way to explain how the particular cognitions can arise, and there will be no way also to explain how there could be any contact of objects with such a formless pure consciousness. According to Kamalaśīla and Śāntarakshita cognition means cognition of objects, and there is no other kind of cognition apart from the changing cognitions of diverse objects. Thus the view of Kumārila that a non-cognitional cognitive activity has to be admitted for explaining the facts of cognition is false, for if the cognition of objects would require another cognitive operation to make itself revealed, then that cognitive operation in the second grade may also require another cognitive operation in the third grade, and so on. It has, therefore, to be admitted that all cognitions are self-revealing, and that they do not require any further cognitive affair to make them revealed.

19. The reason why the idealistic Buddhists hold that knowledge is identical with its object is that when a particular object is manifested in a particular object-cognition invariably manifesting that object, then the object and the cognition must be identical; since blue is always manifested in a blue cognition, all the blue cognitions are identical. Any two things that are simultaneously manifested are identical. This is called the law of simultaneous manifestation (*sahopalambhaniyama*). The blue does not exist objectively outside the blue cognition, and yet it is for the sake of explicitness that it is said as if the blue had existed outside the cognition and that the blue and the blue cognition were simultaneously manifested. The whole idea inherent in this logic is that the awareness and its object have the same revelation; whatever is the apprehension of cognition is also the apprehension of the blue. The opponent of idealists may, however, object that the simultaneous apprehension of the awareness and its object may be due not to their identical character but to other facts of which they are both the joint products. This argument is refuted by Kamalaśīla and Śāntarakshita. They say that if these factors happen simultaneously to the awareness and its objects, then they cannot be regarded as their cause. If, however, they are identical with it, then the Buddhist position that the cognition and its awareness are identical is proved. It is well known that the Buddhists admit only two kinds of position, e.g. that of identity and that of productivity. The idealistic Buddhists do not admit that any of the entities or dharmas can have any kind of activity, and therefore the view that there is a cogniser who cognises the objects, which presupposes an activity, is positively denied. It is the self-revelation of an object-form cognition that is called the apprehension of the cognition. It should not, however, be thought that Śāntarakshita would for a moment tolerate the view that cognitions are actually changed into the form of the objects, or hold any such view in which the objects of the world may be regarded as modifications of some kind of petrified consciousness. All the forms of cognition are ultimately to be regarded as illusory, for even one identical cognition may have (e.g. that of a many coloured flower) many diverse characters revealed in it, and if it be admitted that cognition has no parts, then it is impossible that one cognition should have such diverse characters. It is from this point of view that it has been said that the cognitions have no intrinsic nature of their own and therefore they have no definable nature. This view of Śāntarakshita and Kamalaśīla seems to have been anticipated by Diṅnāga also. For want of proper materials it is at present difficult to say if Śāntarakshita's idealism could in any way be distinguished from that of Diṅnāga, but so much is certain that Diṅnāga also thought that what was subjectively apprehended as the cognised object appeared as if it were an external object, and that therefore such objects of knowledge had their ground and cause in knowledge and knowledge alone. Diṅnāga further thought that each cognition had in it the power by which the subsequent cognition was determined, and it is, of course, difficult for us to say whether Diṅnāga also held, like Śāntarakshita, that there were parallel streams of conscious states without there being a fundamental ground-consciousness as was admitted by Vasubandhu.

20. The great difference between the system of idealism of Śāntarakshita and Kamalaśīla and that of Vasubandhu is that while Vasubandhu admitted the existence of an eternal consciousness and also a consciousness as concrete universal (ālayavijñāna), which was imposed upon it and which formed the ground of the synthesis of each stream of conscious thoughts in their individual aspects, as also in their joint products as determining their mutual intercourse, Śāntarakshita and Kamalaśīla admitted only parallel streams of consciousness without any ground to support them, while each individual cognition had such a dependency of origination in it by which it became associated with categories or relations, and as it passed away it influenced the appearance of other cognitive states, and they in their turn other states, and so on.

21. The Nyāya view of the soul, that our thoughts must have a knower and that our desires and feelings must have some entity in which they may inhere, and that this entity is soul, and that it is the existence of this one soul that explains the fact of the unity of all our conscious states as the experience of one individual, was objected to by Śāntarakshita and Kamalaśīla. They held that no thought or knowledge required any further knower for its illumination; if it had done so, there would be a vicious infinite. Again, desires, feelings, etc. are not like material objects, which would require a receptacle in which they might be placed. The so-called unity of consciousness is due to a false unifying imagination of the momentary states as one. It is also well known that the different entities may be regarded as combined on account of their fulfilling the same kinds of functions. It is knowledge in its aspect of ego that is often described as the self, though there is no objective entity corresponding to it. It is sometimes argued that the existence of the soul is proved because of the fact that a man is living only so long as his vital currents are connected with the soul, and that he dies when they are disconnected from it; but this is false, for unless the existence of soul be proved, the supposition of its connection with the vital currents as determining life is untenable. Some, however, say that the self is directly perceived in experience; if it had been so there would not have been such diversity of opinion about its existence. The sense of ego cannot be said to refer to the self, for the sense of ego is not eternal, as it is supposed to be. On the other hand, it refers sometimes to our body, as when I say I am white; sometimes to the senses, as when I say I am deaf; and sometimes to intellectual states. It cannot be said that its reference to body or to senses is only indirect, for no other permanent and direct realisation of its nature is realised in experience. Feelings, desires, etc. also often arise in succession and cannot therefore be regarded as inhering in a permanent self. The conclusion is that as all material objects are soulless, so also are human beings.

22. Against the Sāṃkhya view of the self, it is pointed out that the Sāṃkhya regards the self as pure consciousness, one and eternal, and as such it ought not to be able to enjoy diverse kinds of experiences. If it is held that enjoyment, etc. all belong to Buddhi and the Purusha only enjoys the reflections in the Buddhi, it may well be objected that if the reflections in the Buddhi are identical with Purusha, then with their change the Purusha also undergoes a change; and if they are different, the Purusha cannot be considered to be their enjoyer. Again, if the Prakṛti concentrates all its activities for the enjoyment of the Purusha, how can it be regarded as unconscious? Again, if all actions and deeds belong to Buddhi, and if Buddhi be different from Purusha, why should the Purusha suffer for what is done by the Buddhi? If, again, by the varying states of pleasure and pain the nature of Purusha cannot be affected, then it cannot be regarded as an enjoyer; and if it could be affected it would itself be changeable.

23. The Upanishadic thinkers hold that it is one eternal consciousness that illusorily appears as objects, and that there is in reality no perceiver and perceived, but only one eternal consciousness. Against this view it is urged by Śāntarakshita and Kamalaśīla that, apart from the individual cognitions of colour, taste, etc., no other eternal, unchangeable consciousness is experienced. If one eternal consciousness is the one reality, then there cannot be a distinction of false knowledge and right knowledge, bondage and emancipation. There being only one reality, there is no right knowledge which need be attained.

24. One of the most important points of Śaṅkara's criticisms of Buddhism is directed against its denial of a permanent soul, which can unite the different psychological constituents or could behave as the enjoyer of experiences and the controller of all thoughts and actions. The Buddhists argue that for production of sense-cognition as the awareness of colour or sound what is required in addition to the sense-data of colour, etc. is the corresponding sense faculties, but the existence of a soul cannot be admitted to be indispensable for this purpose. Vasubandhu argues that what is experienced as the sense-datum of the psychological elements in groups is called skandha. And the individual self (ātman) cannot be anything more than a mere apparent cognitional existence (prajñaptisat) of what in reality is but a conglomeration of psychological elements. Had the apparent self been something as different from the psychological elements as colours are from sounds, it would then be regarded as an individual (pudgala); but if it is different from these psychological elements or its difference be of the same nature as the difference of the constituents of milk from the appearance of milk, then the self could be admitted only to have a cognitional existence. The Vedānta, however, holds that consciousness is entirely different from everything else. So long as the assemblage of any physical or physiological conditions antecedent to the rise of any cognition, as, for instance, the presence of illumination, sense-body-contact, etc., is being prepared there is no knowledge, and it is only at a particular moment that the cognition of an object arises. This cognition is in its nature so much different from each and all the elements constituting the so-called assemblage of conditions that it cannot in any sense be regarded as the product of any collocation of conditions. Consciousness, thus not being a product of anything and not being further reducible to any constituent elements, cannot also be regarded as a momentary flashing. Uncaused and unproduced, it is eternal, infinite and unlimited. The main point on which consciousness differs from everything else is the fact of its self-revelation. The so-called momentary flashing of consciousness is not due to the fact that it is momentary, that it rises into view and is then destroyed at the next moment, but to the fact that the objects that are revealed by it are reflected through it from time to time, and the consciousness is always steady and unchangeable in itself. The immediacy of this consciousness is proved by the fact that though everything else is manifested by coming in touch with it, it itself is never expressed, indicated or manifested by inference or by any other process, but is always self-manifested and self-revealed. Consciousness is one, it is neither identical with its objects nor on the same plane with them as a constituent element. Consciousness cannot be regarded as momentary; for, had it been so, it would have appeared different at every different moment. If it is urged that though different consciousnesses are arising at each different moment, yet on account of extreme similarity this is not noticed, it may be replied that if there is difference between the two consciousnesses of two successive moments, then such difference must be grasped either by a different consciousness or by the same consciousness. In the first alternative the third awareness, which grasped the first two awarenesses and was different, must either be identical with them, and in that case the difference between the three awarenesses would vanish; or it may be different from them, and in that case if another awareness be required to comprehend their difference and that requires another, and so on, there would be a vicious infinite. If the difference itself be said to be identical with the nature of the consciousness, and if there is nothing to apprehend this difference, then the non-appearance of the difference implies the non-appearance of the consciousness itself; for by hypothesis the difference has been held to be identical with the consciousness itself. The non-appearance of difference, implying the non-appearance of consciousness, would mean utter blindness. The difference between the awareness of one moment and another cannot thus either be logically proved or realised in experience, which always testifies to the unity of awareness from the moment of its appearance. It may be held that the appearance of unity is erroneous and that as such it presumes that awarenesses are similar, for without such a similarity there could not have been the erroneous appearance of such an entity. But unless the difference of the awarenesses and their similarity are previously proved, there is nothing which could even suggest that the appearance of unity is erroneous. It cannot be urged that if the existence of difference and similarity between the awarenesses of two different moments could be proved to be false, then only could the appearance of unity be proved to be true; for the appearance of unity is primary and directly proved by experience. Its evidence can be challenged only if the existence of difference between the awarenesses and their similarity be otherwise proved. The unity of awareness is a recognition of the identity of the awareness which is self-evident.

25. Śāntarakshita urges that existence can only be affirmed of those entities which are capable of serving a purpose (*arthakriyā samartha*). He urges that entities can only serve a purpose if they are momentary. Entities that persist cannot serve any purpose and therefore cannot have any existence. In order to prove his thesis he enters into the following argument. If any purpose is to be served then that can either be in succession or simultaneously, and no other middle alternative is possible. If an existing entity persists in time, then all its effects ought to come about simultaneously. If, however, it is objected that even a persisting entity can perform actions in succession owing to its association with successive accessories, then one may well enquire about the nature of the assistance given by the successive accessories to the persisting entity in the production of the effect; is it by producing a special modification of the persisting cause or by independent working in consonance with the productive action of the persisting cause? In the first alternative the special modification may either be identical with or different from the nature of the persisting entity, and both these alternatives are impossible; for if it is identical then, since the effect follows in consequence of the special modification of the accessories, it is the element of the special modification that is to be regarded as the cause of the effect and not the persisting entity. If it is again urged that the effect is due to the association of the special modification with the persisting entity, then it would be impossible to define the nature of such association; for an association may be either of identity or of productivity and neither of them is possible in the present case, as a special modification is recognised for its being different from the persisting entity and is acknowledged by assumption to be produced by the accessories. Again, such association cannot be regarded as being of the nature of inseparable inherence (*samavāya*), for this special modification being of the nature of an additional assistance cannot be regarded as being of the nature of inseparable inherence. If this special modification be regarded as being neither of the nature of an additional assistance nor of the nature of an identical essence with the persisting entity, and if it is still regarded as being associated with the persisting entity in a relation of inseparable inherence, then anything in the world could be regarded as being in relation with anything else. In the other alternative, in which it is maintained that a persisting entity only awaits the independent working of its accessories, it may well be asked whether the causal nature of the persisting entity is the same with the totality of the accessories or different from it. In the former case, the accessories would also be persisting. In the latter case, the persisting entity can no longer be regarded as persisting.

26. The objection against the momentariness of all things on the ground that things are perceived and recognised to be the same and as persisting, is not a valid one. For the fact of persistence cannot be perceived by the senses and must be regarded as due to false imagination. All recognition is due to the operation of memory, which is almost universally recognised as invalid for purposes of right knowledge. On this point it may be argued that in recognition, if the entity now perceived be the same as the entity perceived at a previous time, then how can a cognition in the past comprehend an entity of the present time? If they are held to be different, then it is acknowledged that the entities perceived as the same in recognition are not really the same. The objector's argument, that since things pass by the same name they must be persisting, is invalid; for it is well known that even in ordinary perception, where the flame is known to be destroyed every moment and produced anew, it is still said to be the same flame in common verbal usage. Thus, all existing things must be regarded as momentary. The entire philosophy of later Buddhists depends upon this doctrine of momentariness as its fundamental support, and their quarrel with the Vedānta on the one side and with the realists on the other is very largely based upon their acceptance of this doctrine and its corollary.

27. Śāntarakshita and Kamalaśīla also attempted to refute the categories of substance, qualities, action, class-concepts, specific peculiarities, relation of inherence and other categories of the Nyāya and the Vaiśeshika. Thus, speaking against the eternity of atoms, they hold that since no special excellence can be produced in eternal entities no conditions or collocations of any kind can produce any change in the nature of the atoms; thus the atoms being always the same in nature, either all objects should be produced from it all at once or not at all. The mere fact that no cause of atoms is known is no ground for thinking that they are causeless. Again, substance as different from the characters and qualities is never perceived. The refutation of wholes (*avayavī*), which has already been done, also goes against the acceptance of substantive wholes, and as such the four substances of earth, water, air and fire, which are ordinarily regarded as substantive—wholes made up of atoms—also are untenable. Again, it is not easy to prove the existence of separate and independent time and space-entities, for spatial and temporal determinations may well be explained as mental modifications due, like other facts of experience, to their specific causes. The Buddhists of course accept the existence of manas as an instrument separate from the sense-organs, but they do not admit the existence of manas as an eternal and single entity.

28. The refutation of substance implies the refutation of guṇas or qualities which are supposed to be dependent on substances. If the substances do not exist, there can also be no relation of inherence in which relation the guṇas are supposed to exist in substances. There is again no meaning in accepting colours, etc. as being different from the atoms in which they are supposed to exist. The perception of numbers also ought to be regarded as due to mental modifications associated with particular cognitions. There is no reason to suppose that numbers should stand as separate qualities. In a similar manner, Śāntarakshita and Kamalaśīla proceed with the refutation of the other Nyāya categories.

29. Proceeding with the refutation of action (*karma*), they hold that if all things are admitted to be momentary, then action cannot be attributed to them; for action, involving as it does successive separation of parts and association of contact-points, implies many moments for its execution. If things are admitted to be persisting or eternal, then also movement cannot be explained. If things are admitted to be always moving, then they will be moving while they are perceived to be at rest, which is impossible. If the things are at rest by nature, there cannot be any vibratory movement in them. The main principle involved in the refutation of qualities and karma consists in the fact that the qualities and karma are regarded by the Buddhists as being identical with the particular sense-data cognised. It is wrong, in their view, to analyse the sense-data as being a substance and having qualities and motion inhering in them as different categories. Whatever may be the substance, that is also the quality which is supposed to be inhering in it, as also the motion which it is supposed to have.

30. Regarding the refutation of class-concepts, the main drift of Buddhist argument is that though the perception of class-concepts may be supposed to be due to some causes, yet it is wrong to assume the existence of eternal class-concepts, which exist constantly in all the changing and diverse individual members of a class. For, howsoever we may try to explain it, it is difficult to see how one thing may remain constantly the same, though all the individual members in which it is supposed to exist are constantly changing. If class-concepts are said to inhere, owing to specific qualities, e.g. cooking in the cook, then also it may be objected that since the operation of cooking is different in each case, there is no one character of cooking by virtue of which the class-concept of cook is admissible. Moreover, a cook is called a cook even when he is not cooking. Considerations like these would lead any thinking person to deny the existence of eternal class-concepts.

Chapter VI

THE VEDĀNTA AND KINDRED FORMS OF IDEALISM

1. The most important interpretation of Upanishadic idealism has been that of the Brahmasūtras as expounded by Śaṅkara and as further elaborated by his followers. It has already been pointed out that in the Geetā and in the Pañcarātra literature attempts have been made to interpret the Upanishads in a more or less systematic manner. Interpretations of Upanishadic monism are also found in the Śaiva and Tantra literature to which brief reference will be made in the later parts of this chapter. There seems to be little doubt that these Upanishadic interpretations were very much influenced by the development of Buddhistic Idealism, and we know that Śāntarakshita said that his only point of quarrel with the followers of the Upanishads was in the fact that they admitted one eternal consciousness as the ultimate principle, whereas he admitted only parallel series of consciousness. It may, however, be remembered that there are many important Buddhistic idealists, such as Aśvaghosha, Asaṅga, Vasubandhu, Sthiramati and others, who admitted one eternal consciousness as the ultimate principle. One of the most famous of the Hindu exponents of the Upanishads that preceded Śaṅkara, who was deeply influenced by the Buddhistic Idealism, was Gauḍapāda, who was probably a teacher of Śaṅkara. At the beginning of the fourth chapter of his Kārikās he says that he adores that great man who, by knowledge as wide as the sky, realised that all appearances were like the vacuous sky. He then goes on to say that he adores him who dictated that the

touch of the untouchable (probably referring to nirvāṇa) was the good that produced happiness to all beings, and that he was neither in agreement with this doctrine nor found any contradiction in it. He further says that some disputants hold that coming into being is existence, whereas others quarrelling with them hold that being is non-existence; there are again others who quarrel with them and hold that neither existence nor non-existence is liable to begin and there is only one non-coming into being. Gauḍapāda agrees with those who hold that there is no coming into being.

2. Gauḍapāda thinks that the fourth state of the self as unseen is unrelationable, ungraspable, indefinable, unthinkable, unspeakable and the extinction of the appearance, the quiescent, the good and the One. The world-appearance would have ceased if it had existed, but all this duality is mere māyā (magic or illusion) and it is the One that is ultimately real. In the second chapter Gauḍapāda says that what is meant by calling the world a dream is that all existence is unreal. That which neither exists in the beginning nor in the end cannot be said to exist in the middle. Being unreal, the phenomenon appears as real. The appearance has a beginning and an end and is therefore false. In dreams things are imagined internally, and in the experience that we have when we are awake things are perceived as if existing outside, but all of them are but illusory creations. What is perceived in the mind is perceived as existing at the moment of perception only. External objects are supposed to have two moments of existence (viz. before they are perceived, and when they begin to be perceived), but this is all mere imagination. That which is unmanifested in the mind and that which appears as distinct and manifest outside are all imaginary productions in association with the sense-faculties. There is first the imagination of a perceiver or soul (jīva), and then along

with it the imaginary creations of diverse inner states and the external world. Just as in darkness the rope is imagined to be a snake, so the self is also imagined by its own illusion in diverse forms. There is neither any production nor any destruction. There is no one who is enchained, no one who is striving, no one who wants to be released. Imagination finds itself realised in the non-existent existence of the many and also in the sense of unity; all imagination, either as the many or the one, is false. There is no many nor are things different or non-different. The sages, who have transcended attachment, fear and anger and have gone beyond the depths of the Vedas, have perceived the truth as the imaginationless cessation of all appearance, the one.

3. In the third chapter Gauḍapāda says that reality is like the void (*ākāśa*), which is falsely conceived as taking part in birth and death, coming and going and as existing in all bodies; but howsoever it be conceived, it is all the while not different from ākāśa. All things that appear as compounded are but dreams and māyā. Duality is a distinction imposed upon the One by māyā. The truth is immortal, it cannot therefore by its own nature suffer change. It has no birth; all birth and death, all this manifold are but the result of an imposition of māyā upon it. One mind appears as many in the dream, so also in the waking state one appears as many, but when the mind-activity of yogins is stopped there arises this fearless state, the extinction of all sorrow, final cessation. Thinking everything to be misery, he should stop all desires and enjoyments, and thinking that nothing has any birth, he should not see any production at all. He should awaken the mind into its final dissolution and pacify it when distracted; he should not move it towards diverse objects when it rests in peace. When he neither passes into dissolution nor into destruction, when there is no apprehensible character, no appearance, that is the perfect Brahman.

4. In the fourth chapter Gauḍapāda says that all dharmas (appearances) are without death or decay. He then follows a dialectical form of argument which reminds us of Nāgārjuna. Thus he says that those who regard *kāraṇa* (cause) as the *kārya* (effect in a potential form) cannot consider the cause as truly unproduced, for it suffers production; how can it be called eternal and yet changing? If it is said that things come into being from that which has no production, there is no example by which such a case may be illustrated. Nor can it be considered that anything is born from what has itself suffered production. How, again, can he come to a right conclusion about the regressus ad infinitum of cause and effect? Without reference to the effect there is no cause and without reference to cause there is no effect. Nothing is born either by itself or through others; call it either being, non-being or being-non-being, nothing suffers any birth, neither the cause nor the effect is produced out of its own nature and thus that which has no beginning cannot be said to have any production. All experience and existence are dependent on causal reasons, for otherwise both would vanish. When we look at all things in a connected manner they seem to be dependent, but when we look at them from the point of view of reality or truth, the reason ceases to be reason. The mind does not come in touch with objects and thereby manifest them, for since things do not exist they are not different from their manifestations in knowledge. It is not in any particular case that the mind produces the manifestations of objects while they do not exist, so that it could be said to be an error, for in present, past and future the mind never comes in touch with objects which only appear by reason of their diverse manifestations. Therefore neither the mind nor the objects seen

by it are produced. Those who perceive them to suffer production are really making false impositions on the vacuity. Since the unborn is perceived as being born the essence then is the absence of production, for it being of the nature of absence of production it could never change its nature. Everything has a beginning and an end and is therefore false. The existence of all things is like a magical or illusory elephant and exists only as far as it merely appears or is related to experience. There is thus the appearance of production, movement and things, but the pure knowledge is the unborn, unmoved, the unsubstantial, the cessation. As the movement of burning charcoal is perceived as a straight or curved line of fire, so it is the movement of consciousness that appears as the perceiver and the perceived. All the attributes (e.g. the straight and the curved lines of the fire) are imposed upon the charcoal fire which is neither straight nor curved. So also all the appearances are imposed upon consciousness, though in reality they do not possess it. We could never indicate any kind of causal relation between the consciousness and its appearance, which is therefore to be demonstrated as unthinkable. A thing is the cause of a thing, and that which is not a thing may be the cause of that which is not a thing, for all the appearances are neither things nor those which are not things, so neither an appearance is produced from the mind nor is the mind produced from the appearance. So long as one thinks of cause and effect one has to suffer the cycle of existence, but when that notion ceases there is no such cycle of existence (*saṇsāra*). All things are regarded as being produced from a relative point of view only (*saṃvriti*), and there is therefore nothing permanent. Again, no existent things are produced, hence there cannot be any destruction. Appearances are produced only apparently, not in reality; their coming into being is like māyā, and that māyā again does not exist. All appearances are like shoots of magic coming out of seeds of magic and are not therefore either eternal or destructible. As in dreams or in magic men are born and die, so are all appearances. That which appears as existing from an imaginary point of view is not so in reality, for the existence depending on others, as shown in all relative appearance, is after all not a real existence. That things exist, do not exist, do exist and not-exist and neither exist nor not-exist, that they are moving or steady or none of those, are but thoughts with which fools are deluded.

5. That these doctrines are borrowed from Mādhyamika doctrines of Nāgārjuna and other Vijñānavāda doctrines of the Buddhists is obvious. Gauḍapāda seems to have assimilated all the Buddhistic Śūnyavāda and Vijñānavāda teachings, and thought that these held good of the ultimate truth preached by the Upanishads. It is not out of place here to observe that the Upanishadic passages seem to have inspired Gāuḍapāda. The fourth stage of the self is the one quiescent bliss wherein all appearances have ceased, which is not visible, which cannot be used in ordinary experience, which is unperceivable, indefinable, unthinkable, unnameable, as a mere cognition of a unity seems to suggest a philosophy which is not very far from the doctrines of Buddhist Idealism.

6. The date of the Yogavāsishṭḥa cannot definitely be ascertained, but it seems to me that it cannot be later than the seventh or eighth century. In this work also, which is regarded as a sacred Hindu work, the influence of Buddhistic Idealism is remarkably great. It is interesting to notice briefly some of the special features of the philosophy of Yogavāsisṭḥa to show the extent to which semi-philosophical compositions within the Hindu circle were influenced by Buddhistic ideas. Thus the Yogavāsishṭḥa holds that the world as such never existed in the past, nor exists now, nor will exist hereafter, so it has no production or destruction in any real sense. But yet there is the appearance, and its genesis has somehow to be accounted for. The ultimate entity is indefinite and indescribable, pure extinction or pure intelligence, and remains always in itself and does not really suffer any transformation. Out of the first moment of this entity arises ego, which in spite of its appearance is in reality nothing but the ultimate entity. Gradually, by a series of movements like waves in the air, there springs forth the entire world-appearance. That which appears before us is due to the imagination of mind, like dreams in a fairy-land. There is nothing else except that ultimate entity, and whatever else appears does not exist at all—they are all mere mental creations, proceeding out of the substanceless, essenceless, mental creations of the ultimate entity. The mind again, by whose creations everything springs forth in appearance, has no proper form, and it is merely a name, mere nothingness. It does not exist outside nor subjectively inside us; it is like the vacuity surrounding us everywhere; that anything has come out of it is merely like the production of a mirage stream. All characteristics of form and existence are like momentary imaginations. Whatever appears and seems to have existence is nothing but manas, though this manas itself is merely a hypothetical starting-point having no actual reality. For the manas is not different from the dreams of appearance and cannot be separated from them, just as one cannot separate liquidity from water. Manas is thus nothing but the hypothetical entity from which all the dreams of appearance proceed, though these dreams and manas are but the same and it is impossible to distinguish between them. It is the perceiver which appears as the perceived, and it is but the perceptions which appear as the perceiver and the perceived.

7. The state of emancipation is the cessation of this world-appearance. There is in reality no perceiver, perceived or perceptions, no vacuity, no matter, no spirit or consciousness but pure cessation and pure negation, and this is what we mean by Brahman. Its nature is that of pure cessation and it is this which the Sāṃkhya called Purusha, the Vedāntists Brahman, the Idealistic Buddhists "Pure idea" (*Vijñānamātra*) and the Nihilists "Pure essencelessness" (*Śūnya*). It is described as that essencelessness (*Śūnya*) which does not appear to be so and in which lies the ground and being of the essenceless world-appearance, and which in spite of all creations is essenceless. The illusory world-appearance has to be considered as absolutely non-existent, like the water of a mirage or the son of a barren woman. The ultimate entity is thus neither existent nor non-existent and is both statical and dynamical, indescribable and unnameable, neither being nor non-being, nor being-non-being, nor becoming, but yet some sort of a scheme is offered here for explaining the origin of the world-order. The first moment of the ultimate entity is regarded as something like self-reflecting thought producing some indescribable objectivity giving rise to an ego; on a further movement a state is produced which can be described as a self-thinking entity, which is clear and pure intelligence in which everything may be reflected. It is only this entity which can be called conscious intelligence. As thought-activity becomes more and more concrete other concepts of the soul arise out of it. At this stage it forgets as it were its subject-objectless ultimate state and it wants to flow out of itself as a pure essence or creative movement. The first objectivity is manifested as ākāśa or pure activity and along with it arise the ego and time. This creation is, however, in no sense real, it is nothing but the seeming appearances of the self-conscious movement of the ultimate being.

Thought, which at this moment is like the ākāśa and the ego and which is the seed of all the conceivings of thought, conceives by its movement air, and by a similar process other elements are produced. These are all, however, ideal creations, and as such there is no reality apart from their being as world-appearance. Since their nature is purely conceptual (*vikalpa*), they cannot be real at any time. All that appears as existing does so only as a result of the conceptual activity of thought. There is no single soul, far less an infinite number of them. It is by the all-powerful conceptual activity of Brahman that there arises the appearance of so many centres of subjective thought as the souls. In reality, however, the souls have no other existence than the conceptualising activity which produces their appearances.

8. Manas or mind is essentially of the nature of activity, and the cessation of activity means the destruction of manas. Manas means that activity which subsists between the being and the non-being and induces being through non-being. It is by the activity of manas that the subject-objectless pure consciousness assumes the form of a self-conscious ego. Manas thus consists of this constantly positing activity. It is the synthetic function of manas that is called the functioning of the volitional senses by which all actions are performed, and it is for this reason that *karma* is nothing but manas. The terms *manas*, *buddhi*, *ahaṃkāra*, *citta*, *karma*, *kalpanā*, *saṃsṛti*, *vāsanā*, *vidyā*, *prayatna*, *smṛti*, *indriya*, *prakṛti*, *māyā* and *kriyā* are only different in name, and they create confusion by these varied names; in reality, however, they signify the same concept, namely the active functioning of manas or citta. These different names are current only because they put stress on the different aspects of the same functioning. They do not mean different entities but only different moments, stages or aspects. Thus the first moment of self-con-

scious activity leading to different directions is called manas. When, after an oscillating movement, there is an arrest as "The thus", it is called buddhi. When by the false associations of body and soul there is the feeling of a concrete individual as "I", it is called ahaṃkāra. When there is reflective thought associated with the memory of the past and the anticipation of the future, it is called citta. When the activity is taken in its actual form as notion or action towards any point, it is called karma, and so on.

9. The state of Brahman is higher than the state of manas. It is by becoming manas that Brahman transforms itself into the thought-activity and thus produces the seeming changeful appearances. But Brahman in itself cannot have anything. And though there is this change into manas and through it the production of the world-appearance, yet such a change is illusory and not real, for all the time that this change makes its appearance and seems to stay, Brahman remains shut up within itself absolutely changeless. All the objective appearance is thus nothing but identically the same as Brahman, and all that appears has simply no existence. But the question arises, that if the world-appearance is nothing but the illusory creative conception of manas, how can the order of the world-appearance be explained? The natural answer to such a question in this system is that the seeming correspondence and agreement depend on the similarity of the imaginary products in certain spheres and also on accidents. It is by accident that certain dream series correspond with certain other dream series. But in reality they are all but empty dream constructions of one manas. It is by the dream desires that the so-called physical objects (which in their turn are nothing but dream constructions) gradually get to be considered as steady objects existing outside of us. But though during the continuance of the

dreams they appear to be real they are all the while nothing but mere dream conceptions. The self-alienation by which the pure consciousness constructs the dream conceptions is such that though it always remains identical with itself, yet it seems to posit itself as its other and as diversified by space, time, action and substance.

10. The difference between the ordinary wakeful state and the dream state consists in this, that the former is considered by us as being associated with permanent convictions, whereas the latter is generally thought of as having no permanent basis. Any experience, which is consistent and coherent, comes to be regarded as permanent, whereas if even our waking conceptions come to be regarded as incoherent they lose their validity as representing permanent objects, and our faith in them is shaken. If the dream experiences persisted in time, and the waking experiences were momentary, then the waking state would be considered as a dream and the dream experiences would be considered as ordinary experiences. It is only in the waking state that there is a break of the dream experiences and the waking experiences contradict our dream perceptions and we thus consider the latter to be dreams and therefore to be false. But so long as the dream experiences lasted in the dream state we did not consider them to be false, for during that time these dream experiences appeared somehow to be permanent and therefore real. There is thus no other difference between dream states and waking states, except that the latter are persistent, continuous and permanent, while the former are changeful and discontinuous.

11. It is needless here to deal with the philosophy of the Yogavāsishṭḥa in more detail, but from what has been said it will appear that this system of thought is very much like the idealistic systems of Buddhism that have already been described. If the term manas be replaced by the term ālayavijñāna, then it would be almost indistinguishable from the system of Aśvaghosha or other similar schools of Buddhistic idealism.

12. I would now turn to the interpretation of the Upanishad philosophy by Bādarāyaṇa in his Brahma-sūtra. It seems to me pretty certain, as I shall show elsewhere, that Bādarāyaṇa's philosophy was some kind of Bhedābhedavāda or a theory of transcendence and immanence of Brahman. He seems to have believed that the world was a product of a real transformation of Brahman or rather of his powers and energies (śakti). Brahman himself was not exhausted by such a transformation and always remained as the master creator, who by his play created the world and who could by his own powers destroy the world without any extraneous assistance. The world was thus a real transformation of God's powers, while He Himself though remaining immanent in the world through His powers transcended it at the same time and remained as its controller and rewarded or punished the created mundane souls in accordance with their good or bad deeds. The doctrine of Bhedābhedavāda is certainly prior to Śaṅkara, as it is the dominant view of most of the Purāṇas. It seems probable, also, that Bhartṛprapañca refers to Bodhāyana, who is referred to as Vṛttikāra by Rāmānuja and Vṛttikāra and Upavarṣa by Śaṅkara and Dramiḍācāryya referred to by Śaṅkara and Rāmānuja; all of these held some form of Bhedābheda doctrine. Bhartṛprapañca has been referred to by Śaṅkara in his commentary on the Bṛhadāraṇyaka Upanishad, and Ānandajñāna in his commentary on Śaṅkara's commentary gives a number of extracts from Bhartṛprapañca's commentary on the Bṛhadāraṇyaka, which have been collected by Professor Hiriyanna of Mysore. The doctrine of Bhartṛprapañca is a monism of the Bhedābheda type. The relation between Brahman and the jīva as that between Brahman and the world is one of identity in difference. An implication of this view is that both the jīva and the physical world evolve out of Brahman, and thus his doctrine may well be described as Brahma-pariṇāmavāda. On the spiritual side Brahman is transformed into the antaryāmin (inner controller) and the jīva (soul); on the physical side into *avyakta*, *sūtra*, *virāj* and *devatā*, which are all cosmic. They are all the *avasthāna* or modes of Brahman and represent the classes into which the variety of the universe may be divided. They are again classified into three groups, namely God, soul and matter.

13. It is indeed difficult to say what were the exact characteristics of Bādarāyaṇa's Bhedābheda doctrine of Vedānta, but there is very little doubt that it was some special type of Bhedābheda theory, and even Śaṅkara's own commentary (if we exclude only his parenthetic remarks which are often inconsistent with the general drift of his own commentary and the context of the sūtras) shows that it was so. If, however, it is contended that this view of real transformation is only from a relative point of view, then there must be at least one sūtra where the absolute point of view is given; but no such sūtra has been discovered even by Śaṅkara himself. If experience always shows the causal transformation to be real, then how is one to know that the ultimate points of view of all effects are false and unreal? If, however, it is contended that there is a real transformation of the māyā stuff, whereas Brahman always remains unchanged, and if māyā is regarded as the power of Brahman, how then can the power of Brahman as well as its transformations be regarded as unreal and false, while the possessor of the power is regarded as real and absolute? There is a great diversity of opinion among the Vedāntic writers of the Śaṅkara school; thus the author of Padārthanirṇaya says that Brahman and māyā are both material causes of the world-appearance —Brahman the vivartakāraṇa (unchangeable ground) and the māyā the pariṇāmi cause (the evolutionary material cause). Others find a definition of causation intermediate between vivarta and pariṇāma, by defining material cause as that which can produce effects which are not different from itself. The world is identical with Brahman, inasmuch as it has been and is identical with being, and different from it, inasmuch as it has its characteristics of materiality and change. So from two different points of view both Brahman and māyā are the causes of the world. Vācaspati Miśra holds that māyā is only an accessory cause, as Brahman is the real ground cause (vivarta). Prakāśānanda, the author of Siddhāntamuktāvalī, however thinks that it is the māyā energy which is the material cause of the world and not Brahman. Brahman is the unchangeable and is the support of māyā, and is thus the cause of the world in a remote sense. Sarvajñātmamuni, however, believes Brahman alone to be the vivarta cause, and māyā to be only an instrument for the purpose. The difficulty that many of the sūtras of Bādarāyaṇa give a pariṇāma view of causation was realised by Sarvajñātmamuni, who tried to explain it away by suggesting that the pariṇāma theory was discussed approvingly in the sūtras only because it was nearest to the vivarta theory, and by initiating people to the pariṇāma theory it would be easier to lead them to the vivarta theory. This explanation could have some probability if the arrangement of the sūtras were such as to support the view that the pariṇāma theory was introduced only to prepare the reader's mind for the vivarta view, which was ultimately definitely approved as the true view. But the content of almost all the sūtras of II. I consistently support the pariṇāma view. It is therefore reasonable to suppose that Bādarāyaṇa's interpretation of the Upanishads must have been a Bhedābheda view of some kind.

14. Śaṅkara starts with the premise that whatever may be the reason, it is a fact that all experience starts and moves in an error which identifies the self with the body, the senses or the objects of the senses. All cognitive acts presuppose this illusory identification, for without it the pure self can never behave as a phenomenal knower or perceiver, and without such a perceiver there would be no cognitive act. Śaṅkara does not try to prove philosophically the existence of the pure self as distinct from all other things, for he is satisfied in showing that the Upanishads described the pure self unattached to any kind of impurity as the ultimate truth. This with him is a matter to which no exception can be taken, for it is so revealed in the Upanishads. This point being granted, the next point is that our experience is always based upon an identification of the self with the body, the senses, etc., and the imposition of all phenomenal qualities of pleasure, pain, etc. upon the self; and this with Śaṅkara is the beginningless illusion. All this was said by Gauḍapāda. Śaṅkara accepted Gauḍapāda's conclusions, but did not develop his dialectic for a positive proof of this thesis. He made use of the dialectic only for the refutation of other systems of thought. This being done, he thought that he had nothing more to do than to show that his idea was in agreement with the teachings of the Upanishads. He showed that the Upanishads held that the pure self, as pure being, pure intelligence and pure bliss, was the ultimate truth. This being accepted, the world as it appears could not be real. It must be a mere magic show of illusions of māyā. Śaṅkara never tries to prove that the world is māyā, but accepts it as indisputable. For, if the self is what is ultimately real, the necessary conclusion is that all else is mere illusion or māyā.

Brahman, according to Śaṅkara, is the cause from which proceeds the origin, subsistence or destruction of this world, which is extended in name and form, which includes many agents and enjoyers, which holds the experience of fruits of deeds determined in specific space and time, and following upon definite causes—a world, the formation of which is inconceivable even by the longest imagination of our minds.

15. The reason that Śaṅkara adduces for the existence of Brahman may be considered to be threefold: (1) The world must have been produced as the modification of some thing; but in the Upanishads all other things are spoken of as having originated from something other than Brahman, so Brahman is the cause from which the world has sprung into being, but we could not think that Brahman itself originated from something else, for then we should have a regressus ad infinitum. (2) The world is so orderly that it could not come from an unintelligent source. The intelligent source from which this world has come into being is then Brahman. (3) The Brahman is the immediate consciousness which shines as the self as well as the objects of cognition which the self knows. It is thus the essence of us all, the self; and hence it remains undenied even when one tries to deny it, for even in the denying it shows itself forth. It is the self of us all and is hence ever present to us in all our cognitions.

16. Brahman, according to Śaṅkara, is the identity of pure being, pure intelligence and pure bliss. Brahman is the self of all of us. So long as we are in our ordinary waking state, we are identifying the self with thousands of illusory things, with all that we call "I" or "mine"; but when in dreamless sleep we are absolutely without any touch of these phenomenal notions, the nature of our true state as pure bliss is partially realised. The individual self as it appears is only an appearance; the real truth is the true self, which is one for all as pure intelligence, pure bliss and pure being. All creation is of course illusory māyā, but accepting it as māyā it may be conceived that God created the world as a mere sport. From the true point of view, there is no God who created the world, but in the sense in which the world exists and we all exist as separate individuals we can affirm the existence of God as engaged in creating and maintaining the world. In reality all creation is illusory, and so the creator is also illusory. Brahman itself is at once the material cause as well as the efficient cause of the world. There is no difference between the cause and the effect; the effect is but an illusory imposition on the cause and is thus a mere illusion of name and form. We may mould clay into plates and jugs and call them by so many different names, but it cannot be admitted that they are by that fact anything more than clay; the transformations as plates and jugs are only appearances of name and form. This world, inasmuch as it is but an effect imposed upon the Brahman, is only phenomenally existing as mere objects of name and form; but the cause, the Brahman, is alone the true reality.

17. We may now turn to some other important problems of Vedāntic epistemology. The Vedānta takes a twofold view of things; the first refers to the ultimate reality and the second to appearance. This ultimate reality is pure intelligence, as identical with pure bliss and pure being. This is called ultimately real in the sense that it is regarded as changeless. By pure intelligence the Vedānta does not mean the ordinary cognitional states, for these have a subjective and an objective content which are extraneous to them. It is interesting to contrast this view with that of Śāntarakshita, who believes only in the different cognitional states and also regards subjectivity and objectivity to be extraneous impositions. He thinks that the cognitional entities, having themselves a concreteness, necessitate such impositions, and since he believes in the concreteness and the uniqueness of these cognitional entities he rules out the idea of a permanent intelligence which forms the fundamental thing of the Vedāntic theory of knowledge. According to the Śaṅkara school of Vedānta this pure intelligence is pure immediacy, identical with the fact of the revelation found in all our conscious states. Our apprehensions of objects are in some sense events involving both a subjective and an objective contrast. But their special features in every case are revelatory inwardness or immediacy, which is non-temporal and unchangeable. When I see a blue colour there is a blue object, there is a peculiar revelation of an appearance as blue and the revelation of the eye as the perceiver. The revelation is such that it is both a revelation of a certain character as blue and a certain thing called the blue object. When a revelation occurs in perception it is one and it touches both the object as well as its appearance in a certain character as blue. The revelation is not the product of a certain relation which happens at any time between the self, the character-appearance and the object, for both the character-appearance as blue and the object are given in revelation. The revelation is self-evident and it stands unique by itself. Whether I see, or hear, or feel, the fact remains that there is some sort of an awareness which does not change. Awareness is ever present by itself and is not undergoing the change that its contents undergo. I may remember that I saw a blue object five minutes previously, but when I do this what I perceive is the image of the blue object with a certain temporal and spatial relation which arises or becomes revealed, but the fact of the revelation cannot be revealed again. I may be conscious, but I cannot be conscious of consciousness. For consciousness as such in its immediacy cannot become an object of any other consciousness. There cannot be any such thing as the awareness of an awareness or the awareness of the awareness of an awareness, howsoever we may multiply such phrases in language at our pleasure. When I remember that I have been to Trinity College this morning, this only means that I have an image of the way across the Commons to Church Street and Trinity Street; my movements through them are temporarily pushed backward, but all this is a revelation as an image of the present moment and not a revelation of a past revelation. I cannot say that this present image in any way reveals that particular image as the object of the present revelation; but the former revelation could not be held to be distinct from the present one, for the distinction is always based on content and on revelation. Revelation as such is identical, and since this is so, one revelation cannot be the object of another. It is incorrect to say that "*A* is *A*" means that one *A* becomes itself once again. It is owing to the limitations of the grammatical terminology that identity is thus described. Identity thus understood is different from what one understands by identity of relations. Identity understood as a relation presupposes some difference as "*A* is *A*", and this is not self-contained. And because it is not self-contained it cannot be called relation. When it is said that "*A* is identical with itself", it means that in all the various occasions or contents in which *A* appears it always signifies the same thing. Identity in this sense is the function of thought not existing by itself but in relation to a sense of opposite or otherness. But revelation has no otherness in itself; it is absolutely ubiquitous and homogeneous. And the identity of revelation of which we are speaking does not mean that the revelation signifies the same thing amidst the diversity of contents.

18. It is simply the one essence identical in itself and devoid of any numerical or other kinds of difference. It is absolutely free from "now" and "then", "here" and "there", "such" and "not-such", and "this" and "that". Consciousness of self-shining self taken in this way cannot be regarded as the relation of an appearance to an object, but it is the fact of the revelation or the entity of the self. If we conceive a revelation in this way, it would be an error to make any distinction in revelation as the revelation of the past or the revelation of the present moment, for moments are revealed as objects are revealed; they do not constitute revelation nor affirm any part of it. This revelation is identical with the self-shining self to which everything else has to be related in order to be known.

19. Is cognising an act or a fact? Before this can be answered the point to be made clear is what is meant by cognising. If we ignore the aspect of revelation and speak of mental states which can be looked at from the point of view of temporal or qualitative change of character, we must speak of them as acts or events. If we look at any mental state as possessing certain characters and relations to its objects, we have to speak of it as a fact; but if we look at cognising from the point of view of its ultimate principle and reality as revelation, we cannot call it either an act or a fact, for as revelation, it is unique and unchangeable in itself. All relations and characters are revealed in it, it is self-evident and is at once in and beyond them all. Whether we dream or whether we experience an illusion or a truth, revelation is always there. When we looked at our mental states we found that they were always changing, but this was so only with reference to the contents. But apart from this there is a continuity in our conscious self. By this continuity the Vedānta does not refer to any sort of coherence in our ideas but to the fact of the permanence of revelation. It may be asked, what remains of revelation if the mental states are taken away? The question is not admissible, for the mental states do not form part of revelation; they are rendered conscious by coming into relation with revelation. This category is the ultimate reality. It is not self or subject in the sense in which self or ego is ordinarily understood; for what is ordinarily understood as the ego or the "I" is as much a content of the perception of the moment as any other objective content. It is not impossible that any particular objective content may be revealed at any time without the corresponding "I" being explicitly revealed at the same time. The notion of ego or "I" does not refer to an everlasting abiding self or person, for this notion is as changing as any other objective content. The "I" has no definite real content as referring to an existing entity, but is only a particular mode of mind which is often associated as a relatively abiding content in association with other changing contents of the mind. As such it is changeable as any other object. "I know this" only means that there is a revelation which at one sweep reveals both the "this" and the "I". In such a revelation the revealed "this" and the "I" are manifested in a subjective mental state having a particular conscious centre different from other similar centres. But since revelation cannot in reality be individuated, all that we may say about "I" or "mine", "thou" or "thine" falls outside of it. They are all contents of indefinite existence and revealed by the principle of revelation under certain conditions. This principle of revelation thus has a reality in quite a different sense from that which is used to designate the existence of any other object. All other objects are dependent upon this principle of revelation for their manifestation and their nature or essence cannot be defined or described. They are not self-evident, but are only experienced by coming into some sort of relation with this principle of revelation.

We have already seen that this principle of revelation cannot be either subjective or objective. For all considerations of subject and object fall outside of it and do not in any way qualify it, but are only revealed by it. There are thus two principles: the principle of revelation, and all those which are revealed by it. The principle of revelation is one, for there is nothing else like it; it alone is real in the highest and truest sense. It is absolute in the sense that there is no growth, decay or change in it, and it is perfectly complete in itself. It is infinite, in the sense that no finitude can form part of it, though through it all finitudes are being constantly revealed. It is all-pervading, in the sense that no spatial or temporal limits can be said to affect it in any way, though all these are being constantly revealed by it. It is neither in my head nor in my body nor in the space before me, but yet there is nowhere that it is not. Apart from this principle of revelation, which is called self or ātman or Brahman, all else is constituted of a substanceless, indefinable stuff called māyā.

20. In some schools of Śaṅkara Vedānta called Dṛṣṭi-sṛṣṭi schools, apparently founded on the interpretations of Maṇḍana and later on expounded by Prakāśānanda and others, it is said that all is pure and simple illusion, and that things exist only when they are perceived and dissolve into nothingness as soon as we cease to perceive them. Prakāśānanda tried to show that there were no grounds for holding that external objects existed even when they were not perceived, or that external objects had a reality independent of their perceptions. Examining the capacity of perception as a proof to establish this difference between perception and its object, he argued that since the difference between awareness and its object was a quality of the awareness, the awareness itself was not competent to grasp this quality in the object, as it was one of the constituents of the complex

quality involving a difference of the awareness and its object; to assert the contrary would be a fallacy of self-dependence (*ātmāśraya*). If the apprehended difference is a complex such as difference-between-awareness-and-object, and if this complex is a quality which is apprehended as existing in the object, which has to be assumed in order that the nature of awareness may be realised, it must depend upon itself as a constituent in the complex difference-between-awareness-and-its-object directly and immediately—it comes to the same thing as saying that awareness becomes aware of itself by being aware of itself, which is impossible. If it is held that the complex qualities (difference-of-awareness-from-the-object) are directly sensibly perceived in the object through the senses, then it has to be assumed that the said complex quality existed in the object even before the production of the awareness, and this would involve the impossible supposition that the complex quality of which the awareness was a constituent was already perceived even before such awareness had already come into being. If perception of direct awareness cannot be said to prove the difference between the awareness and its object there can be no inference which may be supposed to do it, for such an inference has to take the following form: "The object is different from its own awareness because it is associated with entirely different kinds of qualities or characteristics". But how could it be known that the object had qualities of an entirely different character from its awareness, since difference between an awareness and its object was contrasted and could not be proved by perceptions or any other means? In proving the invalidity of the supposition that knowledge necessarily implies an object, Prakāśānanda raises the question whether such an implication of an object as conditioning knowledge refers to the production of knowledge, its persistence or its secondary cognition. As regards the first alternative, Prakāśānanda says that, according to the Vedānta, consciousness is ever existent and is never a product, and even if it is regarded as a product, the process of cognition can itself be regarded as the sufficient cause for its production. It can by no means be urged that the presence of an external object is necessary for the production of knowledge in all cases, for, though it is arguable that in perception an object is necessary, no one will suggest that an external object is to be considered necessary in the production of inferential knowledge—a fact which shows that the presence of an external object is not indispensable for the production of knowledge as such. As regards the persistence of knowledge, it is said that awareness has not the object that is known as its locus or support; again, the absence of the object as apart from the awareness would make it impossible for awareness to proceed; and, if knowledge is supposed to be proceeding in anything, that something would not be cognised as object but the cogniser itself—as in the Nyāya view, where knowledge is regarded as an attribute of self and the self is then regarded as the support of knowledge. Since, again, cognition and its object do not exist in the same place or in the same time (this is proved by the possibility of our knowing a past or a future object), there cannot be any such concomitance between the two that it would be right for any one to infer the external presence of any object because of there being a subjective cognition or awareness. So he argues: "There is no proof that cognition and cognised objects are different".

21. In the above account of Prakāśānanda's views it is clear that he does not attempt to give any positive proof in support of his thesis that the world-appearance and all objects contained in it have no existence while they are not perceived, or that the being of all objects cognised is their *percipi*. He only tried to show that it could not be logically established that the awareness of blue and blue were two different objects; or, in other words, it could not be proved that the cognised objects were different from their cognition. The whole universe, as we perceive it, is nothing but cognition without there being any objects corresponding to it. As dreams are nothing but mere awareness without there being any real objects behind them which manifest themselves in different ways of awareness and their objects, so also is the world of waking consciousness. The world has thus no independent substance but is mere cognition and mere awareness.

22. One point that comes out in comparing the idealism of the Śaṅkara school of Vedānta with that of the Buddhists is that though in Vasubandhu's idealism we find that one permanent entity as pure bliss and consciousness is admitted as the ultimate reality, as is also found in this school, yet no attempt has been made in the former to show that this ultimate principle of pure intelligence forms the basic principle of all our consciousness even in our ordinary experiences. In Vasubandhu's system the ultimate consciousness remains largely as the ground principle which remains in its undisturbed quiescence and which is necessary only so far as an unchangeable background is required for explaining all the flux or changes of ordinary experience. In that system it is the ālayavijñāna, or the concrete universal, which is the universal basis of the synthesis of all subject-object creations and their developments, both in the light of each individual stream of consciousness as also in their mutual relations. In the Śaṅkara Vedānta, however, the basic principle of pure intelligence explains the growth of experience in each individual not only as a hypothetical ultimate background but as one that takes part in the formation of each and every one of our experiences; yet this is not all. The so-called external

world of objects is also supposed to be the result of the transformation of the indefinable māyā-stuff on the same basic principle of pure intelligence which forms the ground of our psychological experiences. Thus Prakāśātman in his Pañcapādikāvivaraṇa raises this point and says that the great difference between the Mahāyānists and the Vedāntins consists in the fact that the former hold that the objects have neither any separate existence nor any independent purpose or action, while the latter hold that though the objects are in essence identical with pure consciousness, yet they can fulfil independent purposes or functions and have separate abiding and uncontradicted existence. Both Padmapāda and Prakāśātman argue that since the awareness remains the same while there is a constant variation of its objects and, since, what remains constant and what changes cannot be considered identical, the object cannot be regarded as being only a modification of the idea. The Buddhist idealists urge that if the object (e.g. blue) is different from the awareness it cannot be revealed in it; and if the blue can be revealed in the awareness at that moment all the other things of the world might as well be revealed, for there is no such specific relation with the blue that the blue alone should appear in consciousness at that moment. If it is urged that the blue produces the awareness of the blue, then what would be the function of the visual organ? It is better, therefore, the Buddhists suggest, to admit a natural and unique relation of the identity of the idea and the object. The Vedāntists object to it and say that such a supposition cannot be true, for we perceive that the subject, the object and the idea are not one and the same. To such an objection the Buddhist replies that these three do not form a complex unity which arises at three successive moments of time and then by virtue of their potency or root impression forms a complex of the three; and this complex should not therefore be interpreted as being due to a relationing of three distinct entities. Thus the fact that "I perceived blue" is not to be interpreted as a conscious relationing of "I", "blue" and the "awareness", but as an ideation arising at one particular point of time involving all the three constituents in it. Such a supposition is necessary because all appearances are momentary and because the relationing of the three as three independent entities would necessarily be impossible without the lapse of some time for their operation of relationing. The theory of momentariness only leads us to the above supposition that what appears as relationing is nothing but one momentary flash which has the above three as its constituent elements. So the Buddhist is supposed to admit that psychologically the awareness and its object seem to be different, but such a psychological appearance can at best be considered as a momentary illusion or fiction. For, logically the Buddhist cannot admit that the momentary appearance can subsist long enough to have the possibility of being relationed with the self and the awareness, as in "I know the blue", and if the blue was not considered to be identical with awareness there would remain no way to explain the possibility of the appearance of the blue in the awareness.

23. Padmapāda points out that the main point with the Buddhists is their doctrine of causal efficiency (*arthakriyākāritva*), or the maxim that "that alone exists which can prove its existence by effecting some purpose or action". They held further that this criterion of existence could be satisfied only if all existences were momentary; and if all things are momentary. The only epistemological view that can consistently be accepted is the identity of the awareness and the object. A thing exists because it produces an effect, but the same identical effect cannot be produced twice, so since the

effects are different from their causes the existences must also be different. Padmapāda urges in refutation of it that, if causal efficiency means the productivity of its own awareness, then no awareness or idea has existence, for it does not produce any other knowledge of itself, and the awareness of one cannot be known by others except by inference, which again would not be direct cognition. If causal efficiency means the production of another moment, then the last moment having no other moment to produce would itself be non-existent; and, if the last moment is proved to be non-existent, then necessarily all the other moments would be non-existent. Existence is a nature of things, and even when the thing remains after an operation, it does not on that account cease to exist. On such a basis Prakāśātman points out that the supposed three notions of "I", "awareness" and the "object" are really three distinct notions appearing as one on account of their association, and all the three are joined together in one identical subject-object-awareness, which does not involve the three successive stages as the Buddhist supposes. This identity is proved by the fact that they are recognised to be so. We are, again, all conscious of our identity that we perceive in all our changing states of consciousness and, though our ideas are continually changing with the changing objects, we remain unchanged all the same; and this shows that in knowing ourselves as pure awareness we successively communicate with the changing objects. But the question arises, who is to be convinced of this identity, a notion of which can be produced only by a relationing of the previous experience (through sub-conscious impressions of memory) with the experience of the present moment, as this cannot be done by the Vedāntic self, which is pure self-revealing consciousness, which cannot further be made an object of any other conscious state, for it is unchangeable, indestructible, and there cannot be in it a conscious relationing between the past state and the present state through the sub-conscious impressions of the memory. The mere persistence of the same consciousness is not the recognition of identity, for the recognition of identity is a relation uniting the past as past with the present as present; and since there is no one to perceive the relation of identity the appearance of identity is false.

24. The Vedāntic answer to such an objection is that, though the pure consciousness cannot behave as an individual, yet the same consciousness associated with mind may behave as an individual who can recognise his own identity as well as that of others. The mind, associated with the sub-conscious impressions of a felt ego due to the experience of the self as associated with past time, being responsible for the experience of the self as associated with present time, produces the notion of the identity of the self as persisting both in the past and in the present. A natural objection against such an explanation is that, since the Vedānta does not admit that one awareness can be the object of another awareness, the revival of a past awareness is impossible, without which recognition of identity cannot be explained. The answer of the Vedāntist is that, just as an idea is remembered through its sub-conscious impressions, so, though recognition of identity was absent in the preceding moment, yet it could arise through the operation of the sub-conscious impressions at a later moment. According to the Vedānta, the pure consciousness is the only unchanging substance underlying; it is the consciousness associated with mind that behaves as the knower or the subject, and it is the same consciousness associated with the previous and later time that appears as the objective self with which the identity is felt, and which is known to be identical with the knower—the mind-associated consciousness. We all have notions of self-identity and we feel it as "I am the same"; and the only way in which this can be explained is on the basis of the fact that consciousness, though one and universal, can yet be supposed to perform diverse functions by virtue of the diverse nature of its associations, by which it seems to transform itself as the knower and the thousand varieties of relations, and objects which it knows. The main point which is to be noted in connection with this realisation of the identity of self is that the previous experience and its memory prove that the self existed in the past; but how to prove that what existed is also existing at the present moment? Knowledge of identity of the self is something different from the experience of the self in the past and in the present. But the process consists in this, that the two experiences manifest the self as one identical entity which persisted through both the experiences, and this new experience makes the self known in the aforesaid relation of identity. Again, when I remember a past experience, it is the self as associated with that experience that is remembered. So it is the self as associated with different time relations that is remembered; so, it is the self as associated with the different time relations that is apprehended in an experience of the identity of self.

25. From all these discussions, one thing that comes out clearly is that, according to the Śaṅkara Vedānta as explained by the Vivaraṇa school of Padmapāda and his followers, the sense-data in the objects have an existence independent of their being perceived; and there is also the mind called *antaḥkaraṇa*, which operates in its own ways for the apprehension of this or that object. Are objects already there and presented to the pure consciousness through the mind? But what then are objects? Śaṅkara's answer is that they themselves are unspeakable and undefinable. It is easy to notice the differences of such a view from that of the Buddhistic idealism of Diṅnāga and Laṅkāvatāra on the one hand, and that of Vasubandhu in his Triṃśikā on the other. For, in the case of the former, there are no objects independent of their being perceived, and in the case of the latter, the objects are transformations of a thought principle and are as such objective to the subject. Both the subject and the object are grounded in the higher and superior principle, the principle of thought. This grounding implies that this principle of thought in its transformations is responsible both for the subject and the object, both as regards material and also as regards form. According to Śaṅkara's Vedānta, however, the stuff of world-appearance, mind, the senses, and all their activities, functionings and the like, are but the modifications of māyā, which is indescribable (*anirvācya*) in itself, but which is always related to pure consciousness as its underlying principle and which, in its forms as material objects, hides it (conscious principle) from the view, and is made self-conscious by the illuminating flash of that underlying principle of pure consciousness in its forms as intellectual states or ideas. The Śūnyavādins also admitted the objective existence of all things and appearances, but as these did not stand the test of criticism, they considered them as essenceless. The only difference that one can make out between this doctrine of essencelessness and the doctrine of indescribableness of the Śaṅkara school is that this indescribableness is yet regarded as an indescribable something, as some stuff which undergoes changes and which transforms itself into all the objects of the world. The idealism of the Śaṅkara Vedānta does not believe in the *sahopalambhaniyama* of the Buddhist idealism, that to exist is to be perceived. The world is there, even it be not perceived; it has an objective existence quite independent of my sensations or ideas; but independence of my sensations or ideas is not independence of the consciousness with which it is associated and on which it is dependent. This consciousness is not ordinary psychological thought, but is the principle which underlies all conscious thoughts. This consciousness is independent and self-revealing, because in all conscious thought, the consciousness shines by itself; all else is manifested by this consciousness and, when considered apart from it, is inconceivable and unmeaning. This independent and uncontradicted self-shiningness constitutes being. All beings are pure consciousness and all appearances are imposed on it, as entities which are expressed by references to it, and apart from which they have no conceivable status or meaning. This is so, not only epistemologically or logically, but also ontologically. The object-forms of the world are there as transformations of the indescribable form of māyā, which is not "being", but dependent on "being"; but they can only be expressed when they are reflected in mental states and presented as ideas. Analogies of world-objects with dream-objects or illusions can therefore be taken only as popular examples to make the conception of māyā popularly intelligible; and this gives the Vedāntic idealism its unique position.

26. In the accounts of the Vedāntic theory of perception, according to the Vivaraṇa school, we find that the mind (*antaḥkaraṇa*) has different functions (*vṛtti*), and according to them it has different names, such as *citta* (as a basis of memory), *buddhi* (as synthetical understanding), *saṃśaya* (as doubt), *manas* (as attention) and *ahaṅkāra* (as ego). The antaḥkaraṇa, thus, is considered as a unity of these and other functions. In one of its functions it is supposed to go out of the body, being associated with a particular sense-organ, to an object in the external world, and it is supposed that it takes the shape or form of that particular object, and, when this is done, these two phenomena happen to be at the two poles. On the external pole on account of the mind's falling on the object and taking its shape, the object is revealed; and on the internal pole, there is a revelation or an awareness of that object. Objects exist in the external world as modifications or transformations of the indescribable māyā-stuff, having for their underlying ground one consciousness, which is also the identical ground of our individual selves. But what are these objects? Before the mind is superimposed upon them they are unknowable. It is through the superimposition of the mind that the unknowable characters of the objects are removed and the objects as constituted by the māyā shine forth through the underlying principle of the consciousness which was their inner nucleus; and precisely the same phenomenon takes place at the internal pole, where the inner consciousness reveals the character of the particular shape or form which the mind has taken, such that the particular perception of the object internally shines forth as an awareness. In the case of illusions also, certain illusory objects are actually created in association with certain physical and mental conditions, and then this illusorily created object has for the time being the same status as an ordinary object, and its perception takes place in the same manner in which the perception of ordinary objects takes place. When the pure consciousness is taken in association with mind, it is called an individual self; it then behaves as a function of the mind, what is called in our ordinary language "I". With reference, however, to the other functionings, modifications or operations of the mind, either as objective forms, or as ideas, or as feelings, it is the ground-consciousness that reveals them and, in this capacity, this ground-consciousness is called the transcendent perceiver (*sākṣī caitanya*). Owing to the differences of mental conditions, previous history of the mental life and other reasons, the revelations of the mental ideas or feelings or objects are sometimes identical with that particular mental function (in association with the ground-consciousness) which appears as "I", or as merely coupled with it as its experience or in other specifications with it. It is on this account that though the manner of revelation is more or less the same, yet experiences show themselves as "I am happy" or "this is a chair" or "I perceive a chair". Both the mind and the external objects are productions of the māyā-stuff on the underlying reality of pure consciousness or Brahman. In the ordinary phenomenal view, therefore, we have on one side the mind, and on the other side the external objects, then we have the superimposition of the mind on the external objects, which may be called the cognising activity, as a result of which there are, on the one hand, the mental images or ideas—which are immediately intelligible by the ground-consciousness—and on the other hand, revelations of the external objects as different from the diverse kinds of ideas, images or awareness.

27. But if this is so, what constitutes the idealism of the Vedānta? The Vedāntic reply to this question is, firstly, that all cognitions are only possible when the identity of the consciousness underlying the self and the external objects is established by the superimposition of the mind on the object, by which process the indescribable and obscure nature of the external objects is removed and diverse objects are revealed both as subjective ideas and as objective entities; secondly, all mental phenomena and the mental entities, and objective phenomena and the objective entities, have as their ultimate essence and reality the pure consciousness; thirdly, in each act of cognition, the mind's association with the external objects modifies its nature to such an extent as to transform it from its indescribable and unknowable nature to cognised forms of awareness. There is also a view that this unity of subjective states with objective entities takes place in the cosmic consciousness of God. It may well be remembered in this connection that God is regarded as a material and instrumental cause of the universe and as such there cannot be anything which is beyond His consciousness. So we have on the one hand the transcendental consciousness as the ultimate reality of everything subjective and objective, and on the other hand God's phenomenal consciousness as the basis or the plane on which all subjective and objective phenomena happen and in which they are manifested.

28. We have seen that all the world-appearances, subjective and objective, are due to the operations of beginningless avidyā or nescience; but when once the instrumentality of this avidyā power is admitted, there is also another element which, though a product of avidyā, may yet be regarded as occupying an important position, at least, as a sub-agent for the production of world-experiences. This may be described as a pragmatical element, called in Sanskrit *arthārthisaṃbandha*. This means that the notions of desiring something, and of having those things by which they are satisfied, go a great way in determining our subjective ideas and our objective findings in the external world. In our treatment of Buddhist idealism, we know that the Vāsanā theory plays a most important part in the construction of world-experience. Avidyā, or ignorance, is no doubt the root cause, but in the field of experience, the importance of vāsanās as the motive power by which diverse categories and relations are invented and utilised for the construction of world-experience cannot be over-estimated. But vāsanās mean nothing more than the root desires which want to create a field in which they may be fulfilled. In the Vedānta also this idea is not abrogated; and side by side with the motive power of avidyā, we have this germ of voluntaristic idealism which is largely due to our root desires, which want to fulfil themselves by certain kinds of constructions. Cessation of desires, the control of the senses in their operation in objective fields, disinclinations to worldly enjoyment, love for emancipation are regarded as fundamental conditions for the study of Vedānta. There is no doubt that it is the power of avidyā by which indescribable forms and entities are created both in the external world and in the subjective field, but yet what remains unexplained is the matter by which the two are brought into co-operation for the construction of world-experience. This is explained on the basis of desires, volitions by which various kinds of relations and various kinds of interpretations and judgments of value take place, so that the data of experience are worked upon for the formation of a concrete experience. This experience remains unconsciously in the mind at each new birth and is further worked upon by fresh desires and volitions, so that the accumulated experiences of past lives become more and more complex by the operation of the present desires and volitions, and in this way we have a complex fabric of mental experiences involving old residues of past experiences in association with new experiences.

29. So far we have only described two different schools of Śaṅkara Vedānta, namely, that of the Dṛṣṭisṛṣṭi school of Maṇḍana, Prakāśānanda and others, and the Vivaraṇa school of Padmapāda, Prakāśātman and others; but there is also another important school, known as Ekajīvavāda. It holds that in association with ignorance, the Brahman or pure consciousness appears as a superintendent, and through the influence of the same ignorance thinks himself as different individuals of the world, connected with separate bodies and undergoing separate experiences in these different individual centres. The individuals have no different minds, but they appear to behave as persons having different minds through the operation of the principle of ignorance, as associated with the superintendent. It is to the functioning of this one principle of ignorance of the superintendent, that diverse persons continue to have their separate illusions, cognitions, feelings, volitions, etc. and also have different histories of their individual experiences. These individuals are therefore like dream-creations proceeding out of the ignorance of this one superindividual. No salvation, however, can be attained by any individual of the world until and unless the one superindividual, who manifests himself through the diverse world-individuals, is himself dissociated from his own ignorance. But yet each individual may proceed on his own way for the attainment of salvation, as he goes on with the other experiences. All these world-individuals are thus nothing but magic creations of this one super-individual.

30. Different Vedāntic teachers have attempted to clarify the meaning of falsehood and the meaning of māyā, which are rather loosely used in Śaṅkara's works. We know that the Buddhists admitted three kinds of existence: (1) ultimate reality (*paramārthasattva*); (2) ordinary phenomenal existence of ordinary experience (called *saṃvṛtisattva* by the Buddhists and *vyāvahārikasattva* by the Vedāntists); (3) illusory existence (Bhrama); (4) a fourth kind of existence is also pointed out which may be described as an impossible concept, which is technically called *tuccha* (e.g. round square or a hare's horn). In the consideration of all these four kinds of existence, Śaṅkara was in all probability influenced by the Buddhistic writers. But Śaṅkara did not properly explain what he meant by saying that the world was false. Padmapāda, a direct disciple of Śaṅkara, draws a distinction between two meanings of falsehood (*mithyā*), namely, falsehood as single negation (*apahṇava vacana*) and falsehood as the unspeakable and indescribable (*anirvacanīyatā vacana*). It is probably he who of all the interpreters first described ajñāna or avidyā as being of a material nature (*jaḍātmikā*) and of the nature of a power (*jaḍātmikā avidyā-śakti*), and interpreted Śaṅkara's phrase "*mithyājñānanimitta*" as meaning that it is this material power of ajñāna that is the constitutive or the material cause of the world-appearances. Prakāśātman, however, elaborates the conception further in his attempts to give proofs in support of the view that avidyā is something positive (*bhāvarūpa*).

31. Vācaspati also believed in avidyā as an objective entity of an indescribable nature, into which all products disappear during the great dissolution (*mahāpralaya*) and out of which they reappear at the end of mahāpralaya and become associated with psychological ignorance and wrong impressions which merge into it at the time of mahāpralaya. (Compare the *prakṛti* of Yoga.) Sarvajñātma Muni holds that the avidyā or ajñāna is positive in its nature, and this character of it is manifested in the world in its materiality and in ourselves as ignorance. But, though it rests in the pure Brahman, yet like butter in contact with fire, it also melts away by his touch in certain conditions. He further holds that Brahman, in association and jointly with ajñāna, cannot be regarded as the material cause of the world. The ajñāna is only a secondary means without which the transformation of appearances is indeed not possible, yet it has no share in the ultimate cause that underlies them. Ānandabodha held that since the appearances cannot be explained without the assumption of a cause which forms its substance, and since also this world-appearance is unreal and cannot therefore come out of substance that is real, and since it cannot come out of something which is absolutely non-existent and unreal, the cause of the world-appearance can neither be real, nor unreal. We are bound, therefore, to accept the hypothesis that the cause of the world-appearance is neither real, nor unreal; and this neither-real-nor-unreal entity is avidyā. Citsukha defines falsity (*mithyātva*) as the non-existence of a thing in that which is considered to be its cause. So, the falsity of the world consists in the fact that it is supposed to be existing as real, though it does not exist—the reality being Brahman alone. He defines the ajñāna or avidyā as a positive entity, without beginning, which disappears with the rise of true knowledge. This avidyā or ajñāna is different from the conception of the positivity as well as of negativity, yet it is called positive only because of the fact that it is not negative. It is described by him as a positive state and not a mere negation of knowledge; and so it is said that the rise of true knowledge of any subject in a person destroys the positive entities of ignorance with reference to that object, and this ignorance is something different from what one would understand by negation of right knowledge. Citsukha further says that the positive character of ignorance is perceived, when we say that "We do not know, if what you say is true". Here there is the right knowledge of the fact that what is said is known, but it is not known, if what is said is true. Here there is a positive knowledge of ignorance of fact, which is not the same as mere absence of knowledge. Such ignorance, however, is not perceived through sense-contact, or through other processes, but directly by the self-revealing consciousness—the *sākṣī*.

32. There have also been many attempts by the later followers of Śaṅkara to disprove the truth of world-appearance; firstly, by challenging all means of proof such as perception, inference, etc. as given by the realists (naiyāyikas); secondly, by refuting all categories and relations as enumerated by the realists, by an application of the dialectic method of logic, more or less on lines similar to that of Nāgārjuna. This method was started on the Vedāntic lines, first by Gauḍapāda, then in a limited manner by Śaṅkara, and then by Śaṅkara's direct disciple Maṅḍana, who wrote an elaborate refutation of the categories of difference, showing thereby that the concept of difference and plurality is self-contradictory. This subject has been treated in the second volume of my *History of Indian Philosophy* and need not be discussed here. Of the many writers, who followed the line of Vedāntic dialectics, four names stand out as very prominent, namely Śrīharṣa, Citsukha, Ānandajñāna and Nṛsiṃhāśrama.

33. The most important philosophical contribution of Śrīharṣa was his Khaṇḍanakhaṇḍakhādya, in which he attempted to refute all the definitions of the Nyāya system intended to justify the reality of the categories of experience, and tried to show that the world and all world-experiences are purely phenomenal and have no reality behind them. The only reality is the self-luminous Brahman or pure consciousness. His polemic is against the Nyāya, which holds that whatever is known has well-defined real existence, and Śrīharṣa's main point is to prove that all that is known is indefinable and unreal, being only of a phenomenal nature and having only a relative existence based on practical behaviour, customs and conveniences. But though it is a polemic against the Nyāya, yet, since its criticisms are of a destructive nature, they could be used, with modifications, equally effectively against other realistic systems. Both Śrīharṣa and the Nihilists (Śūnyavādins) are interested in the refutation of all definitions as such. Śrīharṣa starts with the proposition that none of our awarenesses ever stands in need of being further known nor are they capable of being the objects of any further act of knowledge. The difference of Vedāntists from some of the idealistic Buddhists consists in this, that the latter hold that everything is unreal and indefinable, not even excepting cognitions; but the Vedānta makes an exception of cognition and holds that everything else, excepting knowledge or awareness, is itself indefinable either as existing or non-existing, and is unreal. This concept of māyā is slightly different from the concept of māyā as interpreted by Ānandabodha and others, who regarded it as both existing and non-existing. This indefinableness in the nature of all things in the world and all experiences is such that no amount of ingenuity or scholarship can succeed in defining it. Śrīharṣa undertakes to show that all definitions of things and categories as urged by realistic writers are absolutely hollow and faulty, even according to the canons of logical discussions and definitions accepted by them. If no definition can stand, it necessarily follows that there cannot be any possible definition of the world and that the world of phenomena and all our so-called experiences of it are indefinable. So the Vedāntist can say that the unreality of the world is proved. It is useless for anyone to attempt to find out what is true by resorting to arguments; for the arguments can be proved to be false even by the canons on which they are based. If anyone, however, says that the arguments of Śrīharṣa are open to the same objection and are not true, then this would only establish his own contention; for Śrīharṣa does not believe in the reality of his arguments and enters into them without any assumption as to their reality or unreality. Among the various arguments, that are introduced by Śrīharṣa to prove the reality of the ultimate oneness, there is one argument which may be regarded as an ontological argument and is not very commonly adduced by other writers. Thus Śrīharṣa says that the very demand in our mind for ultimate oneness proves that the idea of ultimate oneness already exists, for if the idea is not realised, no one could think of asking for a proof of it. But it may be said that this idea of oneness is contradicted in perceptual experience which reveals multiplicity of things and their differences, and to this Śrīharṣa replies that neither differences nor different things can exist. By an application of logical dialectic, he tries to prove that the notion of difference or of different things is self-contradictory, and so also is the notion of otherness and mutual negation. He then criticises the notion of right knowledge in its various aspects as perception, inference, implication and the like. He also criticises the realistic definitions of cause and effect, substance, qualities and other categories. Thus, for example, speaking of relations, Śrīharṣa points out that if relation is to be conceived as something subsisting in a thing, then its meaning is unintelligible. The meaning of relation as "in" or "herein" is not at all clear; for the notion of something being a container is dependent on the notion or concept of "in" or "herein", and that concept again depends on the notion of a container and there is no other notion which can explain either of the concepts independently. The containers cannot be supposed to be inherent cause, for, in that case, such examples as "there is a grape in this vessel" or "absence of horns in the hare" would be inexplicable. So he goes on and refutes diverse kinds of conceivable relations, actions, numbers, etc.

34. Citsukha carries on the work of Śrīharṣa with even more acuteness, and discovers many new arguments for refuting all realistic categories of time, space, substance, quality, etc., and all conceivable kinds of relations, class concepts, etc. It is needless for me here to go into details of this dialectical criticism, as this has already been done in the second volume of my *History of Indian Philosophy*.

35. It is not out of place here to mention that the main difference between the dialectic of Nāgārjuna and that of Śrīharṣa, Citsukha and others consists in this, that Nāgārjuna and his followers have no thesis of their own to prove, and so the question whether their thesis is supported by valid proof or not is absolutely immaterial. But though the attitude of the Vedāntic dialecticians was inspired by the Mādhyamikas, yet the whole object of their proving the nullity and falsehood of the world-appearances was for upholding the doctrine of Brahman, the pure consciousness, as the ultimate reality. This ultimate reality as pure consciousness is not only the basis or ground on which all world-creation has evolved, but it is also the ultimate subjective ground on which mind (which limits all our phenomenal experiences by limiting the scope of the infinite consciousness) has evolved as māyā transformations. But this pure consciousness, which can never be grasped as an idea, or image or a particular cognition, always reveals itself in its immediacy in all our phenomenal knowledge. In its aspect as *sākṣī caitanya* it perceives all phenomenal forms when they are cognised and also when they are hidden (previous to mind-object contact, which raise them to the cognitive status) by ignorance. In such a stage it is the ignorance itself that is perceived, as when one says that "I perceive nothing". Here it is the "nothing" that directly becomes the object of sākṣi consciousness.

36. Two main forms are noticeable in the Vedāntic Idealism of Śaṇkara and his followers. Firstly, that of pure subjective idealism as that of Prakāśānanda and the Ekajivavāda already described, and secondly of absolute idealism as that which has been accepted more or less for the fundamental interpretation of the Vedānta through the centuries as initiated by Padmapāda, Prakāśātman and others, which is known as the Vivaraṇa school.

37. Many systems of thought grew up which followed in the main the former idealism that we find in the philosophy of Śaṅkara and his followers. Thus, turning to the Tantra metaphysic, we find that the world is in one sense as unreal and illusory as in Vedānta, for it owes its existence to the connection of māyā with Brahman, but the māyā is here not an unspeakable entity but possesses as much reality as the Brahman or rather is identical with it. Here the ultimate category, the *Śiva*, is *prakāśa*, pure illumination, or abstract self-shining thought, and *Śakti* is *vimarṣa*, or the inherent activity of thought. Thought and its inherent activity cannot be viewed as distinct from each other as the one is involved in the notion of the other. The conception of the nature of thought involves its own activity. That which appears in its abstraction as pure prakāśa in one aspect or moment appears in its other aspect as vimarṣa at another moment. This conception may, therefore, be explained after the Sāṃkhya attempt of the identification of Mahat or Buddhi with Purusha. There we read that the Mahat or Buddhi, as it resembles the pure character of the Purusha, can stand in such a relation to it that the prakāśa is pure, and Mahat being *sattvaguṇamaya* is also pure and, as such, they mutually reflect each other and are identified. The two are, however, different, and this illusory identification is the cause of the production of the world-order. But here we find that prakāśa is imaged in vimarṣa, which stands as a reflector which reflects the real nature of the prakāśa. Prakāśa comes to know of its own true nature only when it perceives itself as reflected through its *kriyā-śakti* or vimarṣa. Abstract thought as such cannot posit its true nature. It is only when it returns to itself through its own movement, kriyā or vimarṣa, that it can posit itself and manifest itself as the "egohood". The first point is the point of prakāśa, the second is the point of the vimarṣa and the third point is the unity of them both, the return of the prakāśa through vimarṣa as the "egohood". The first point in Tantra is called the "white" *bindu*, the second "red", and the third "black". The conception of this action of unification is only that of differentiation in the integrated. The one unperturbed whole holds within itself the aspect of prakāśa, vimarṣa and their unification as the "egohood". This unperturbed whole is called in the Tantra the *mahābindu*. In the Vedānta also the ego (ahaṃ) springs out of the unification of Brahman with māyā. But there māyā is conceived as unreal and so the unity is also unreal; but here the vimarṣa is conceived as being involved in the reality of the prakāśa, through which the prakāśa reflects itself or returns back to itself and realises itself as the ego. In analogy with the *vikṣepa-śakti* of māyā here also we find the *āvaraṇa-devatas*, but these are conceived here as the real transformations of the śakti in its process of self-development.

38. But one of the most interesting systems of idealism approaching Śaṅkara's idealism is that of the Kāshmira School of Śaivism as described in the Śivasūtras and the works of Kṣemarāja, Abhinavagupta and others. According to these systems pure consciousness is ultimate reality which is self-spontaneous, and it is this self-spontaneity of itself that is called māyā. It is this self-spontaneous pure consciousness that manifests itself as the inner psychological categories and the objective presentations that form the data of objective perception. The world-creation is not thus a creation of the indescribable māyā-stuff which has for its ground the changeless Brahman, but it is the pure consciousness which, while remaining unchanged in itself, makes the appearances on itself through its powers, which though not different from it yet show themselves as it were different from it. So, the world-appearance is not false, only it is to be remembered that it is but the manifestation of one pure consciousness. It is by limiting its one infinite consciousness that it appears as individual perceivers. This limitation, again, is not something different from the nature of this pure consciousness, but only a mode of it. The mind, also, is not something different from this pure consciousness; but when the pure consciousness limits itself, then it manifests itself in two ways: firstly, when its limiting function is in ascendancy, it appears as mind, and secondly, when its limiting function is subordinated to its manifesting side, it appears as the revealing consciousness. In the second alternative again, it has modes which are manifested as cognition and as cogniser. In the first alternative it appears as the mind and the external and internal objects of perception, "blue", "pleasure", etc. So even in the case of the so-called world-perception and world-reality, which are regarded as imaginary, we have nothing unreal but only the modes of the real. The world of matter and that of mind are thus both equally spiritual, only their spirituality is manifested in different grades of perfection. Their imperfection does not imply any new element, such as māyā or avidyā, but is to be viewed as the direct product of the limiting activity of the ultimate reality, which is again identified with itself. It is by this limiting activity that the infinite and ultimate reality appears finite, and instead of omniscience we have the scanty knowledge of individual beings, and instead of omnipotence we have the limited will power of man. But even in its limited nature the ultimate reality continues to perform its own functions in a limited manner; thus instead of infinite illumination we have the illumination of specific objects (e.g. blue) in specific time and place and the non-illumination of that entity in other specific times and places. It also posits definite sense-data and illuminates the differences and assimilates them in one consciousness. The problem of the cognition of external objects, such as diverse sense-data, and of internal entities, as pleasure, pain, etc., is explained on the supposition that it is out of the spontaneity of pure consciousness that diverse kinds of objects are manifested to its limited expressions as individual persons. External cognition does not imply that its cause is something external, it only means that being inside the limited consciousness of the individual, the infinite consciousness manifests the limited forms of sense-objects through its own spontaneity. So, it is not necessary to admit any external world independent of the pure consciousness; nor is it right to say that the external world is the product of another entity in association with the ultimate consciousness, for after all it is through the spontaneity of the ultimate consciousness that the illumination of all objects is made possible.

39. I have already indicated that the interpretations of the Upanishads on the monistic line had already been made by various writers long before Śaṅkara. Much of the dialectics of the reasoning of Śaṅkara and of his followers and the whole doctrine of māyā and the fourfold classification of existence, and the theory of Brahman as the ultimate reality and ground, were anticipated by the idealistic Buddhists, and looked at from that point of view there would be very little which could be regarded as original in Śaṅkara; but still one fundamental doctrine of Śaṅkara could be regarded as in some sense original, viz. that there was one reality, the Brahman, which appeared in all its diverse appearances which were all false, whereas Brahman alone was the one reality. This view of causation was regarded as *vivarta* (where the effects are false and the cause alone is true as opposed to the *pariṇāma* view of causation where the changes were as real as the cause); even this view was not only anticipated by some forms of veda vāda view which preceded Śaṅkara, but also by Bhartrihari, who preceded Śaṅkara by about a century, in his Bākyapadiya. It is supposed that the philosophy of Bhartrihari was based on various discussions of metaphysical subjects that are to be found in Patañjali's Mahābhāṣya, but we cannot say how far this contention is right. So far, however, it can be said that Bhartrihari gives us a philosophy in which one being or reality as Brahman is regarded as the ultimate truth and everything else is considered to be mere appearances. So far as these appearances were concerned Bhartrihari was quite willing to accept the ordinary realistic view (which Śaṅkara refuses to do, e.g. class-concepts and the like), but from the ultimate point of view Bhartrihari would not for a moment admit the existence of anything else but the ultimate being. Bhartrihari thinks that it is by the power of Brahman that all these various manifestations, such as individual subjects, the objects and all the relations that appear, have to be explained, yet that power is not in its nature different from the nature of Brahman. For whatever appears has the fundamental characteristic of manifestation, and this would be impossible if they were not themselves also ultimately of the nature of Brahman. The difference of the world of appearances consists only in the fact that for the time being it appears to have its nature as Brahman completely subordinated, and instead of having itself manifested as Brahman it appears only as material objects. It is the one reality that in our eyes associated with ignorance appears as many and limited in space and time and in relation. Just as pure non-being has no differential characteristic from pure being, so succession also has no differential character from pure duration or simultaneity. In the conception of time also, we see that there is one time that is diversely interpreted as succession, simultaneity and is associated with other entities in such forms as existence in past, present or future; but the formless time has none of these characteristics, and it is only by false impositions that we introduce temporal difference in one undivided entity. In this way Bhartrihari criticises all possible categories of qualities, relations, time, space, position, negation, etc. and shows them to be self-contradictory and, therefore, nothing more than false impositions. What remains absolutely unshaken is the pure being which alone is ultimately real.

40. I omit from my present discourse all those systems of thought, such as that of Rāmānuja, Nimbārka, Gopāla Bhaṭṭa or Jīvagoswāmī and Malla, which, according to our definition, should have been taken up as idealistic schools in some sense or other. I have done so not only because my course here is very limited, but also because of the fact that though these systems may in some sense be regarded as idealistic they have in them an undeniable tinge of realism also, and it depends on the interpreter on which side the emphasis is to be given. I have, therefore, taken the liberty of dealing briefly only with those systems which may be regarded to be absolutely idealistic. In the course of these chapters I have tried to show how from the imperfect germs of idealism in the Upanishads different systems of idealism sprang up through the influence of other tendencies that grew with time. Some of them may be called evolutionary idealism, objective idealism, subjective idealism, absolute idealism and also nihilistic idealism, the latter form being almost unknown in European philosophy. I have no doubt not finished here the entire course of the development of the idealism in Indian philosophy, for systems which may be

regarded as idealistic realism or realistic idealism, and those which have found favour in vernacular writers, have not even been touched. Idealism has not only been one of the most dominant phases of Indian thought in metaphysics, epistemology and dialectics, but it has also very largely influenced the growth of Indian ideal as a whole. These subjects, however, may be left open for a future occasion.

INDEX